Your Elephant's Under Threat

How to tap into the transformative power of positive change that eludes you and your business

John Mulry, MSc

Foreword by:

Nick Nanton

Emmy Award Winning Director/Producer and

Best-Selling Author

John Mulry, MSc

Hi Pádraig,

Hope you enjoy the book, look forward to welcoming you into the world of GKIC and the Expect Success Academy!

John Mulry

What others are saying about this book:

"If you're an entrepreneur who's struggling to adapt to the changing world of business or you need a system for defining and getting exactly what you want in life, then you need this book."

-Brian Tracy, Legendary Speaker, Trainer and Author of over 60 Best Selling Books

"Just going through the first part of the book has made me realize a lot of things and I think John's really onto something. The concepts and stories to illustrate them reached into my head and dredged up a few things I'd been keeping to myself, which isn't a bad thing - if the reader takes this information to heart and reads the book several times, it will definitely help him or her to be where they want to be. Having read it, I believe I'll be able to tame the chaos around here as well as in my mind. I have to say, I am totally blown away by all of the information in this book. VERY awesome stuff! I am definitely enjoying this book more than most. Thanks again, John, for choosing me to be your editor; I don't come across books that strike me this much very often, so it's a wonderful thing!"

–Jennifer-Crystal Johnson, Editor and Author of *The Ten Pillars of a Happy Relationship*
www.JenniferCrystalJohnson.com

"What a fantastic, straightforward, and honest book backed by a wonderful story of positive change. If you are an ambitious entrepreneur and want to have your own story of personal triumph and business success, read this book!"

–Clate Mask, CEO and Co-Founder of InfusionSoft

"In order to achieve success in life, you must first expect it, define it, and apply knowledge gained through education and experience. John Mulry's book, *Your Elephant's Under Threat*, is an excellent tool to use on your journey."

–Tom Hopkins, Tom Hopkins International, Speaker and Author of *How to Master the Art of Selling*

"The thing about John that most people aren't willing to do, is to actually apply the best practices that they learn to their own business and life in order to achieve maximum effectiveness in minimum time. I love the fact that John lives and breathes what he teaches in this book. One of the most important concepts that surfaces in his book is summarized in his three words: invest, consume, and act. If ever there was a simple definition of how to succeed, John has 'nailed it' with these words. Moreover, he's living proof that the invest/consume/act model works."

-Nick Nanton, CEO of the Dicks + Nanton Celebrity Branding® Agency, Emmy Award Winning Director, Producer & Best-Selling Author

"I was extremely impressed with this book. John's brutal honesty and acknowledgement of his own mistakes and the unselfish nature in which he is willing to relive past experiences, both good and bad, at least one of which I'm sure you'll relate to is truly commendable. This man is willing to put himself, his story and his vision out there for the sake of others and this sets him apart from the rest. This coupled with the strategies and structures he provides to embrace change and achieve your business goals makes this book a must read and one that I look forward to revisiting over and over."

-Kenny Cosgrove, Milk Marketing

Your Elephant's Under Threat

John Mulry, MSc

Copyright © 2013 by John Mulry

All rights reserved. No part of this book may be reproduced or transmitted in any form or by any means, electronic or mechanical, including photocopying, recording or by any information storage and retrieval system, without written permission from the author, except for the inclusion of brief quotations in a review. This publication is designed to provide accurate and authoritative information in regard to the subject matter covered. It is sold with the understanding that the publisher is not engaged in rendering legal, accounting or other professional services. If legal advice or other expert assistance is required, the services of a competent professional person should be sought.

ISBN-13: 978-0-9928003-0-7

Your Elephant's Under Threat is available at special quantity discounts for bulk purchases, for sales promotions, premiums, fundraising, and educational use. For more information, please write to the below address.

Published by: Expect Success Academy
Unit 14, Ballybane Enterprise Centre
Galway, Ireland

www.JohnMulry.com

First Edition, 2013

Edited by: Jennifer-Crystal Johnson
www.JenniferCrystalJohnson.com

Foreword by: Nick Nanton, Esq.
www.NickNanton.com

Cover Art by: Cory Wright

Published in Ireland

Your Elephant's Under Threat

For Mam and Dad...

To Mam, my biggest fan and my rock. I would be lost without you. I owe you everything and without you I would be nothing – you've taught me so much. Every day I learn something from you and your kindness; your love and support knows no bounds and I treasure all the things you do, great or small.

To Dad, I'll be forever grateful for your love and dedication to raising and providing for us. Through your own hardship and struggles I learned a lot about life, change, and myself. Your pain and suffering was my inspiration, the catalyst to cause me to change for the better. I promised you on your last day here I would do you proud and I'll continue to keep it. Forever your son.

John Mulry, MSc

In life, you don't necessarily get what you want and you don't necessarily get what you need. Instead, you get what you honestly and truly believe you deserve. In other words, you get what you expect, so why not expect success?

–John Mulry

Check out the bonus material details on page 173 for worksheets, larger illustrations, and expert interview downloads.

Acknowledgements

A special mention must go to Jess, my girlfriend, best friend, and reason why. The idea for this book has been there for some time. However, without your love, support, feedback, and guidance, it would still be just an idea. Love you, Jess.

I would also like to acknowledge my coach David Keane, who has helped me realise my own potential to evolve and grow. You've instilled even more belief in me and played a big role in helping me develop as a coach.

I'd like to also acknowledge my clients who, while they may have benefitted radically from me, it pales in comparison to what I have learned from them. In particular, people like Liam Bluett, Kevin Nugent, and Sean Gallagher: your knowledge and expertise in your respective fields has helped me hone my skills and learning from you is as enjoyable as coaching you.

To my sister Liz, thank you for your constant interest, support, praise, and for keeping me grounded.

To Nick Nanton, your own continuous success is something I admire greatly; you have the rare ability of sharing your expertise in a way that empowers business owners to be the best and get the best from themselves and their business. You inspired me to see the true value in my own story, experience, and expertise, and helped me put my thoughts into words.

To Dax Moy, Brian Grasso, and Paul Chubbuck, your contributions to this book must also be noted. Dax, I learn from you every day and thank you for teaching me the principles I wrote about in this book. Brian, you're proof of the success you can have from living with audacity; and Paul, your insight into releasing the past tied everything together.

To my editor Jen, thank you for doing a fantastic job in making my thoughts and words coherent and readable, enjoyable even.

To Cory, your design work speaks for itself.

To everyone who contributed to the 'What is Success' chapter: this book wouldn't be the same without you. In no particular order:

Liam Bluett
Cora Molloy
Jessica Thompson
Kevin Nugent
Conor O Sullivan
Kenny Cosgrove
Michael Smyth
Debbie Gettler
Christine Rianne
Brian Grasso
Christine Rianne
Mark Whitehand
Peter Walkom
Jorgen Anderson
Colman Collins
Stephen Hardiman
Kevin Newell
Sean Gallagher
Declan Loy
Ashling Devlin
Jon McCarty
Brianna Hatswell
Aidan Whelan
Annette Clark
Dawn Arduini Watson
Sheila Lally

Table of Contents

Acknowledgements	9
Table of Contents	11
Foreword by Nick Nanton	13
How to Read This Book	17
Prologue	19
1: This isn't a Self-Help Book	23
2: The Beginning	29
3: Two Special Words	33
4: ESA	35
5: What is Success?	41
6: Change	51
7: South America – The Year That Changed Everything	55
8: Hardship	61
9: Dad	65
10: Fitness and Fetishes	69
11: Loser	73
12: Expect Success	77
13: I was Part of the Problem	79
14: Four Important Points	83
15: Long-Term Versus Short-Term	89
16: Define, Refine, and Align	100
17: It's Not All Mindset, It's Brainset Too	103
18: Basic Define, Refine, and Align Pathway	111
19: Advanced Define, Refine, and Align Pathway	117
20: Three Kinds of People	143
21: Bringing Everything Together	151
22: Doing it Alone	153
23: The Power of Coaching	155
24: What Can the Expect Success Academy Do for You?	159
25: Need Additional Help?	167
26: Resources	171
27: Bonus Downloads	173
28: Bonus Interview with Paul Chubbuck	175
29: Bonus Interview with Dax Moy	193

30: Bonus Interview with Brian Grasso	211
31: The Missing Chapter	225
32: Frequently Asked Questions for John and the Expect Success Academy	229
Additional Praise for John and the Expect Success Academy	233
About the Author	235

Your Elephant's Under Threat

Foreword by Nick Nanton

When John asked me to write this foreword, I was not only eager to help, but also felt proud to do so. Proud? Why?

While I am happy that John credits me and my teachings for playing a role in the unfolding of his story and his career, I am even more excited to see the transformation I have seen John undergo in his own life. I'm proud to be a part of his success to this point and I'm more than a little excited about the great future I see ahead for John and the Expect Success Academy.

The story that follows in this book – of how someone from a small city in Ireland looked outside of his current circumstances for inspiration, guidance, and direction – is one with a familiar ring to it, but trust me, you've never seen the twists and turns you are about to experience when you go on this journey with John. From feeling lost, alone, depressed, and directionless to achieving great success and impacting the lives of many, John has shown that he is a true "transformer" – not only in his own life, but in the lives of his clients as well.

I have spent time with John on a couple of occasions through my speaking engagements in Birmingham, England at Aston University. The events were entrepreneurial and small business owner 'bootcamps' of sorts. The fact that John attends these types of events is a testament to his commitment to lifelong learning and continuously developing himself and his business. This is certainly a key catalyst in John's evolution, not only as a business owner, but also as a coach to others. Moreover, at these events, John isn't just an attendee who sits and takes copious notes (although he does that, too!), but he actively engages in the conversation, contributes, networks, and adds value. These are all important elements in his growth, but perhaps the one gift John has that is probably the most apparent is his gift to find and connect with the experts who have achieved what he wants to achieve, ask the right questions, and implement the key strategies.

John seeks out experts like Dax Moy, Brian Grasso, Jon le Tocq, and others (myself included) and commits to investing in and learning from experts like Dan Kennedy, Brian Tracy, and Tom Hopkins so he can emulate what we are doing to get to the next level. The thing about John that most people aren't willing to do, is to actually *apply* the best practices that they learn to their own business and life in order to achieve maximum effectiveness in minimum time. I love the fact that John lives and breathes what he teaches in this book.

One of the most important concepts that surface in his book is summarized in three words: *invest, consume,* and *act*. If ever there was a simple definition of how to succeed, John has 'nailed it' with these words. Moreover, he's living proof that the *invest/consume/act* model works.

Much like John, out of college I, too, came to a crossroads in my life. I decided to invest in myself, consume and use the resources, coaches, and mentors I invested in, and then I acted upon what I learned. I've never heard it put quite so concisely, but this simple formula of *invest, consume,* and *act* is what led me to the career I am enjoying today.

If it wasn't for *investing, consuming,* and *acting,* I wouldn't have had the opportunity to work with some of the most talented, brightest, and successful experts in the world! Experts like Dan Kennedy, Brian Tracy, Michael Gerber, Jack Canfield, Tom Hopkins, and Dr. Nido Quebin, to name just a few. If I hadn't committed to defining, refining, and aligning what I really wanted in life, like John talks about in this book, I certainly wouldn't have had the opportunity to co-author more than 30 Best-Selling books, get to positively influence thousands of entrepreneurs and professionals around the world through my speaking engagements, or get to share life-changing lessons and experiences through directing documentaries and TV shows.

So, in reading this book I pose a challenge to you. I challenge you to read it openly, draw inspiration from John's fascinating story, immerse yourself in the "define, refine, and align" model for change, and most importantly, act upon what you learn. Don't be afraid! Remember, it's much easier to change the course of a ship that is in motion than to propel it from its berth!

As John says, we only have a small amount of time on this earth, so why not set out expecting success rather than failure. And if you get stuck along the way, there's no need to fret. John and the Expect Success Academy can show you how to unlock the untapped potential in your life and business.

Now, all you have to do is turn the page and get ready to start your journey!

My best wishes for your success,

Nick Nanton - CEO of the Dicks + Nanton Celebrity Branding® Agency, Emmy Award Winning Director & Producer
Best-Selling Author
www.DNAgency.com

John Mulry, MSc

How to Read this Book

With a lot of personal development books, you will often find that you can revisit chapters when you need to. This book is no different. However, I recommend you read this book through at least once to get a full overview of everything contained.

The book details my own story of change, struggle, and triumph, all of which contain valuable lessons you can and will likely relate to. I would suggest reading this with an open mind. Some of the material I present to you here may be new and seem a little out there. It's important when being presented with new information that you don't dismiss it because you have not encountered it before.

Within some chapters there are questions and exercises that you should take time to digest and answer. This will help solidify what you are reading and enable you to take in and retain more information.

The beauty of this book is that, once you have read through it in its entirety, you will be able to revisit each of the chapters as you go through the Define, Refine, and Align stages yourself. This makes it easier to focus on each step as it happens.

I wanted to make this book as actionable as possible because, as you'll discover, I'm a big believer in investing, consuming, and most importantly, acting on what you consume. The worst thing you can do is read this book through once and then let it sit idly on your bookshelf. Think of it as more of an action plan or workbook than a typical book.

A word of caution: typically the percentage of people that implement what they read is low. On average if you take 100 people who read a book, 80 of those will do nothing with the information, 15 will implement some and achieve some success, and 5 will implement everything and go on to great success. I challenge you to break this law of averages and go forth with the intention of implementation.

Throughout the book I mention some other books and resources that have had a positive impact on me and that I highly recommend you read if you haven't done so already.

These resources will be summarised in a resources section at the back of the book also.

> Finally, if you feel that you need help implementing or acting upon what you read, do not hesitate to reach out to me or my Expect Success Academy products and coaching. Visit www.JohnMulry.com to get started.

Prologue

"CHOOSE not to accept the false boundaries and limitations created by the past."

– Unknown

One Bite at a Time

One bite at a time. That's what they tell us. That's how we're supposed to do it. Tackle our problems, I mean. Achieve our goals. We need to break the big, massive problem into small, manageable, bite-size chunks.

You know the saying, "How do you eat an elephant? One bite at a time." And it works. Most of the time.

I'm a problem solver at heart – I guess that's why I am in the business of helping people. It's my calling. I guess it's why I love the world of personal development so much. The notion of breaking down a problem – be it an abstract equation or a problem in life or business – into manageable chunks seems doable. Most of the time.

There's that phrase again, *most of the time*. There are two problems with our elephants and two problems with the bite-size problem-solving formula.

First problem: Elephants never forget. Have you ever had a goal that, no matter what you tried, you just couldn't achieve it? Even if you tried to break it down to the smallest chunks possible? Me, too. It's really frustrating. You start to feel like a failure, like you're not moving forward, like you're regressing instead of progressing.

It's not because you're stupid, it's not because you don't have the time, energy, or resources; it's because your goal or elephant, if you may, is under threat. A threat that won't be forgotten and one that must be addressed.

That elephant you want to break into manageable chunks won't be broken down until you identify the threat behind it that's stopping you from achieving. From there, it's all about Defining, Refining, and Aligning, as Dax Moy calls it.

The second problem with elephants is they're easily conditioned. Let me illustrate with a story. You may have heard of this one. It's not new. It's the story about the elephant and the tether. I first came across this story while devouring every book and seminar by the charismatic and wonderfully talented Tom Hopkins.

A family is out on a day trip to the zoo. It's a glorious summer day and the clear, blue sky is cloudless. The family – a mother, a father, and two young kids – are going from enclosure to enclosure, soaking up the spectacular views of the animals and their antics.

They come upon the elephant enclosure and the father is suddenly on edge. The enclosure is only secured by a measly wire fence and the giant elephant inside is kept there by a small rope held in place by an even smaller wooden stake.

Fearful for his children's safety, he calls over the zookeeper and exclaims, "How on earth can you keep that elephant from going on a rampage and harming little kids?"

The zookeeper laughs and says, "The elephant isn't going anywhere. It's tied down."

"But it's only a thin piece of rope; even I could break free from that," the father says.

"Sure you could, but the elephant can't," the zookeeper replies in a smug voice.

"How can that be?" the father asks.

The zookeeper proceeds to tell the family that when the baby elephants are first put into the enclosure, they are kept there by a big, massive chain that's connected to an even bigger rock.

The baby elephant tugs and tugs at the rope all day, every day but never breaks free. After about six months, it gives up. Completely. At this stage, the zookeepers remove the big chain and rock and replace it with the thin piece of rope and small wooden stake.

To the elephant, it's the same thing. It doesn't matter what's keeping him tied down because he's never going to break free. Why? Because he doesn't believe he can. He's been conditioned to believe he'll never be able to do so.

The same goes for all of us. We all have similar tethers or threats in our own lives that prevent us from moving forward, from living the life we deserve, having a body we can be proud of, and running a business that serves us.

The tethers and threats in our lives aren't just belief-related, either. Other threats can be fear-based, including fear of failure, fear of judgement, fear of commitment, and even fear of success. Anything that holds us back is exactly like the stake keeping the elephant tied down. No matter what size it may be in reality, it's the affect it has on our ability to act that matters most.

Until we address the tethers or threats in our lives, we will never break free and will always be like the elephant that's tied down.

This book aims to help you realise that the threat holding you back in your life and in your business is merely a small piece of rope. I aim to show you that it is one which *you* have the power and answers inside to break free from permanently.

John Mulry, MSc

- 1 -

This Isn't a Self-Help Book

"Whatever the mind of man can conceive and believe, it can achieve."

–Napoleon Hill

First, I should say congratulations. You hold in your hands the keys to positive change. I urge you to go forward and invest in yourself so you, too, can discover how to get everything you want in life and business. If you're reading this book I'm guessing there's some part of your life or business you want to change.

I guarantee you if you draw inspiration from my story and invest in, consume, and act upon the little known secrets I'm about to show you in this book, you will succeed, no question about it.

Whether you're interested in changing your business or career, your health or physical appearance, or any other area of your life, you're in good hands. Alternately, if you're reading this book because I forced you to buy a copy, then that's ok, too.

Now that you have this book, do you have what it takes to read it, apply it, and begin achieving everything you deserve?

I'm guessing you do... if you're currently having doubts, don't worry; that's completely normal. I mean you're probably thinking the last thing you need is another self-help or personal development book, right? Brian Grasso, someone whom I admire and have learned an awful lot from, says that the whole idea of self-help is flawed. He believes that the words 'self-help' indicate that we are broken. I agree with Brian: you are not broken, perhaps you're just lost. This book aims to help show you the way. I interviewed Brian as part of this book and

I've included it along with two others to help you better grasp the concepts and apply them.

In reading, you will be taking some baby steps and some giant ones; the hardest part is taking action. By reading this book, you've started the process. The most important part after this is the follow-through. Reading isn't enough anymore. You need to put what you learn into action.

How many books have you read? How many have you put into use? That's the kicker.

One of the first lessons I ever learned about change is that knowledge *isn't* power. *Applied knowledge* is. One of my mentors, and someone who I'll probably mention more than once in this book, is Dax Moy. He taught me that you can have all the knowledge in the world, but if you don't apply it then it's useless.

In this book you're going to realise that I don't hide anything, I wear my heart on my sleeve, and I'm not afraid to let you into my own story, battles, past successes, and past failures.

You'll discover that I firmly believe that one of the best ways you can achieve your goals is by modelling yourself after people who have gone before you, also known as standing on the shoulders of giants.

When it comes down to it, you already know a lot about what you *should* be doing....

When it comes to positive change and achieving a life you can be proud of:

- You know working smart is better than sitting on your backside.
- You know that you have to be willing grab hold of opportunity and not expect success to be handed to you.

- You know that negative thinking is going to hold you back.
- You know that you should eat right and avoid junk.
- You know that exercise helps you look and feel great.
- You know that, in order to succeed, you have to work smart and be persistent.
- You know that the combination of a healthy mind, body, and spirit are the keys to your success.

The thing is if you know all this, which I'm sure you do (most of it anyway), then how come you're not happy with your current level of success? I mean… you know all of this, surely knowledge is power, right?

Wrong.

Knowledge isn't power; *applied knowledge* is power.

You can have all the knowledge in the world, but if you don't *use* that knowledge then it's pretty much useless.

This is where my book shines.

The problem with success, personal development, and self-help books, courses, and programs is a lot of them tell you what you already know.

Don't get me wrong. I love them. I'm addicted (seriously) to anything related to personal development and self-improvement so I practically consume everything I can on achieving success and personal development.

Everything from Napoleon Hill's *Think and Grow Rich* and *Science of Personal Achievement*, to Tony Robbins' *Personal Power*, and other resources from Tom Hopkins, Brian Tracy, Bob Proctor, Michael Gerber, Brendan Burchard, Brian Grasso, Jay Abraham, Dan Kennedy, Marlon Sanders, Dax Moy, and many, many more.

Similarly to the amazing Tony Robbins, I like to call myself a hunter of success. I crave it and want to know everything about it.

In fact, to this day, my biggest hobby apart from spending time with my beautiful girlfriend, Jess, is investing, consuming, and acting on personal development and self-improvement books, courses, audio programs, seminars, masterminds, and certifications.

Those three words above, "invest, consume, and act," are actually key words in your success – it comes back to the 90%/10% rule which I'll be discussing in detail later on in the book.

The reason why I love these books so much is because they tell you everything you need to know about success. Everything except one thing: the underlying reasons why you can't do what you already know you should be doing.

This book is going to be your catalyst to start applying the knowledge you already have (and the knowledge I'm going to teach you). It's not that hard, you just need that *oomph*, that guy in your corner rooting for you. I can be that guy if you let me.

You may know the things I listed above, and you may even know what I'm about to share with you. The information isn't necessarily new. I'm not claiming to have invented it. I have simply pulled together everything I've picked up from other experts and resources and presenting it in a way that will help you tackle the number one reason holding you back.

With the information in this book, I'll be showing you how you can turn that KNOW-ledge into DO-ledge and start acting on what you know, thus starting a flood of momentum that will lead to you achieving whatever it is that you want to achieve.

I'm going to be showing you some stuff that is *evolutionary*. The word "revolutionary" gets thrown around a lot, but if you actually think about the word revolution, it essentially refers to going around in full circle. In this book and through the Expect Success Academy, what I will be showing you is evolutionary, because if you follow through and take action on what you learn, you'll be taking your life and business to a whole new level. Hence, evolutionary. Tall claim, I know.

What I'll be sharing with you may just scare you and excite you at the same time.

You'll discover how, just a few short years ago, I was completely lost and alone (and was too afraid to tell anyone about it). In fact, as we go deeper, you'll see how even when I was younger, I was always coming up short and never felt like I fit in anywhere. And I'll tell you how my father's own struggles helped me realise how and why I needed to succeed.

It wasn't easy. But as the saying goes, most things worth getting are never easy. If it were, everyone would do it.

It all started here….

John Mulry, MSc

- 2 -

The Beginning

"Your time is limited, so don't waste it living someone else's life."

–Steve Jobs

I always knew I'd be a shepherd. Not in the literal sense, but in the sense that I knew I would be a leader. One that people would seek direction from. Seek guidance, inspiration, and answers from.

Up until a few years ago, I was the furthest thing from a shepherd. I was the proverbial sheep. My whole life had been run by someone else's dream, someone else's goals. I would do things because I was expected to do so. That word, 'expect,' has become something sacred to me, along with another word: success. Those words in combination came much later, though.

I was doing what I thought was expected of me, what I was supposed to do. As you'll discover, growing up for me wasn't exactly a walk in the park. Don't get me wrong, I had a wonderful, loving family and great friends, but I always felt like I was different. I was fascinated by the world outside of Galway, outside of Ireland, and always looked to places like America for inspiration. My sister was the same in that respect. We both have a fascination with everything America-related.

In school, I always tried to go about my business and fit in. As you'll find out, this didn't always go as planned. I was bullied, big time, to the point where I kept my voice hidden and locked up for fear of being ridiculed more. I did what everyone else did, even if I didn't agree with it. Other kids were skipping school, so I'd skip school, too.

Same could be said about alcohol and trouble. I always hung around with guys a little older than me. Guess I wanted to fit in with the cooler guys. I did what they did because it's what I was supposed to do, right?

Same in college, I did what everyone else did, still hiding my true voice. It's funny, when I was in secondary school, I had a meeting with my guidance counsellor, Mr. Honan, and he asked me what I wanted to do. I said I wanted to be successful.

Yes, but what do you want to *do*? I didn't know. We went through a series of exercises and Mr. Honan said something to me that I'll never forget.

He said, "John, you have the rare ability that you can do whatever you want and you'll be successful." Now, whether he said that to everyone or not I don't know, and honestly it doesn't matter.

Whatever I want? I still didn't know what that was. After I left school, I worked for a year before going on to college. I completed the access course in NUI Galway and was in the top 5%, studying subjects I didn't really want to study.

In the first year, mathematics and economics were the goal, simply because it seemed like a great field to get into. I always liked maths and never studied economics but thought, *hey, I'll give it a whirl*. Gary, one of the guys I was friends with in the access course, was doing it – so I said sure, I'll do it, too.

Still following someone else's path, not my own. College was fantastic and I thoroughly enjoyed my time there, had my degree in the bag, and now what? Well, everyone else was doing a masters, so I said I'll do one, too.

Finance, that's where you make the big money, that's what I'll do. Right, off to DCU to get my MSc in Finance, Capital Markets, and business. Then off to London. Investment Banking, here I come. This, too, was someone else's dream, not mine.

And I had no problems getting interviews, all while most of the other guys in my class were struggling to get them. Getting them wasn't the problem. I had interviews in Dublin, Galway, London, Birmingham, and all for the most reputable businesses, too. Barclays, Fidelity, Icap, and the like.

The problem was that I somehow managed to sabotage myself each and every time. I thought I was just not hireable and wasn't suitable. And at some level, that was probably true. I've now to come to realise that I was purposely self-sabotaging because investment banking and finance wasn't the path for me. It was something else entirely.

I did eventually secure a position in Galway and in fact come within a week of doing what so many other young, aspiring, and enthusiastic fresh-out-of-college people do: emigrate.

I decided that if I didn't get a job soon I'd go off to Korea and teach English. Again, lots of people were doing it so I said, you know what, I'll do that, too. Again, following someone else's dream, not my own.

Luckily it never came to that and I secured a position as a business analyst with Boston Scientific. This was my second stint at Boston Scientific, as I had previously worked there the summer after I finished school.

My time at Boston Scientific was pretty uneventful. Apart from dressing up as the Joker in my first week, I pretty much went through the motions at that job and was thoroughly uninspired.

Proinnsias, one of my great friends from college, was living in London at the time and he was also growing disillusioned with 'the real world.' I was going through some major changes as all my work over the last few years seemed like it was for nothing. I was completely lost and didn't know where I was going in life. Was this normal? If it was, it sure as hell shouldn't be.

Proinnsias and I decided we'd both head off somewhere and get our heads straight. This time I said to Proinnsias, "We're going to do something that's not normal, against the grain." I was sick of dong what everyone else did. It was time to do what *I* wanted.

"Where will we go?" he asked.

"Not Australia, not Canada, and not America. Everyone goes to those places. I know, we'll go to South America. I don't know anyone that's ever gone there...."

That, as you'll discover, was one of the best decisions of my life.

- 3 -

Two Special Words

"Definiteness of purpose is the starting point of all achievement."

–W. Clement Stone

I mentioned that there are two words that are very close to my heart. These two words epitomise everything I stand for and everything my mission stands for. You can probably guess what they are, given the name of my business.

"Expect," and, "Success."

Those two words, along with my 'tag line' that goes with them, really solidify everything I stand for. The choosing of those two words came about quite quickly, but I know deep down that the reasoning behind them was something that was playing on my mind for some time.

One of the first (and still one of the best) fitness books I ever read was by the brilliant and natural bodybuilder, Tom Venuto. I studied and studied Tom's book and read it cover to cover multiple times. I also acted upon what I learned and that's where my budding fitness lifestyle change came about initially: through Tom's book.

One of Tom's many sayings in the book was that we must train hard and expect success. It really resonated with me on a deep, deep level.

The reason why is that all through my life up until this point I wasn't expecting anything other than failure. I had no real confidence in myself and my abilities.

Also, I was always doing things because I believed other people expected them from me; I wasn't doing these things for myself, but for other people.

Here was this guy in absolutely amazing shape telling me that I could do it, too. Nobody ever told me that before.

Secondly, whether we like to admit it or not, we as an Irish nation are some of the most pessimistic and negative people there are. Unfortunately it's true, if someone is all enthusiastic and happy, we suspect they are up to something – or worse, they are *on* something.

Maybe this was the reason that I looked so much to America for my inspiration. Americans in contrast are some of the most enthusiastic and upbeat people you'll come across.

Now this may be a generalisation, but the fact of the matter was I chose to look to America for my inspiration instead of somewhere local, and that choice led me to discover the Expect Success mentality, which is something I've tried to embody every day since.

Where have you looked in the past for inspiration? Have you questioned yourself as to why you've looked there?

I remember the day I was thinking of a name for my business, and it came to me immediately: Expect Success Fitness. It has now evolved into the Expect Success Academy.

- 4 -

ESA

"Whatever you can do, or dream you can, begin it. Boldness has genius, power, and magic in it."

–Johann Wolfgang von Goethe

Remember, you don't necessarily get what you want and you don't necessarily get what you need. Instead, you get what you honestly and truly believe you deserve. In other words, you get what you expect, so why not expect success?

That's it for me, everything in one little paragraph. It's funny, it was by reading Michael E. Gerber's wonderful book, *The E-Myth Revisited*, and acting on some of his questions that made me fully realise the power of the mission I had created for myself.

Do you believe in coincidence? I certainly don't. Was it coincidence that I started training a guy called Kenny who was an excellent business plan strategist just at the same time that I needed to redevelop my own? Was it a coincidence that I was reading Michael E. Gerber's book when David, my coach, asked me what my true mission in life was? I don't think so.

You see, however unlinked they may appear, they are linked. In the book *The E-Myth Revisited*, Michael poses a question that is one of the most profound questions you can ever ask yourself.

I took the time to answer this question in depth and a wave of calm, purpose, and sense of direction came over me. It's a difficult question to answer but one worth thinking about, answering, and sharing.

Thankfully, I requested to repeat that question for you today and Michael gladly agreed.

I'd like you to imagine that you are about to attend one of the most important occasions of your life.

It will be held in a room sufficiently large to seat all of your friends, your family, your business associates – anyone and everyone to whom you are important and who is important to you.

Can you see it?

The walls are draped with deep golden tapestries. The lighting is subdued, soft, casting a warm glow on the faces of your expectant guests. Their chairs are handsomely upholstered in a golden fabric that matches the tapestries. The golden carpeting is deeply piled.

At the front of the room is a dais, and on the dais a large, beautifully decorated table, with candles burning at either end.

On the table, in the center, is the object of everyone's attention. A large, shining, ornate box. And in the box is... you! Stiff as the proverbial board.

Do you see yourself lying in the box, not a dry eye in the room?

Now, listen.

From the four corners of the room comes a tape recording of your voice. Can you hear it? You're addressing your guests. You're telling them the story of your life.

How would you like that story to go?

That's your Primary Aim.

What would you like to be able to say about your life after it's too late to do anything about it?

> That's your Primary Aim.
>
> If you were to write a script for the tape to be played for the mourners at your funeral, how would you like it to read?
>
> That's your Primary Aim.
>
> And once you've created the script, all you need to do is make it come true.

Isn't that one of the most thought-provoking questions you could ever answer? If you're serious about achieving personal success, I highly recommend you read Michael's profound book, *The E-Myth Revisited*, and answer that question with complete honesty. You might just find what you're looking for.

When you answer it, the next question becomes not, "how?" or, "what?" It becomes, "why?"

When I answered it, I was looking into the future, looking back on what I have achieved.

Here's my answer in its original form:

> Here you all are, and for that I thank you; those of you who are here really are the most important people in my life. My family, my forever beautiful Jess, our gorgeous and talented kids and adorable dogs (and cats), and close friends – I'd like to thank you for shaping me into the person I am and helping define my life.
>
> To Jess: the moment I met you was one of our many defining moments, but for me it was the beginning of my journey of discovering my true reason why. You have been and always will be that why.
>
> So my life, eh?

Those words, "my life;" I guess it's easy for me to say this given that I'm in a box, but looking back, looking back through my life, there was one thing I wanted, one thing, and that was to leave a legacy, leave something behind, something that would continue to grow and flourish long after I've come and gone, long after the dust has settled. It has never been my aim to coast through life as average. There's nothing inherently wrong with being average; it's just not what I wanted my life to be and I've always strived to show people they shouldn't, either. For me, I wanted people to remember who I was and what I was about long after I've passed.

So what's my legacy? What was my purpose? Well, hopefully by now it's been realised and hopefully, for just one of you sitting or standing, I've influenced you in some positive way.

My legacy has always been to be recognised as someone, an authority in the art of instilling and inspiring personal fulfilment and success... instilling that attitude where you not only want success, but you expect it.

I hope I've inspired and positively influenced you to become the best you that you can be because that's all I've ever wanted for myself, to be the best me I could ever be. Not necessarily the best at any one thing, I just wanted to be the best John Mulry.

I guess looking back I hope I've instilled that, "I can have that, too," attitude and, like so many other greats out there like Robbins, Tracy, Gerber, Canfield, Maltz, Hopkins, Carnegie, Hill, Grasso, Kennedy, Moy, Sanders, I can hold my head high in the knowledge that, in my own way, I've helped shape just one of you into the best you that you can be.

It's funny, there are many blessings being born Irish but one of them isn't our ability to be sceptical; we second guess everything, so it's kind of funny that it all started with two words: "expect success." They began with fitness but soon outgrew that to plant the expect success seeds in all areas of my life including business, personal success, and relationships.

Those two words can epitomise how I strived to live my live, my creed for life, and looking back, if you were to sum up my life's legacy, it would come down to my desire to show people how to "expect success" in every area of life.

It's short-lived, our time on this little globe, so why not set out every day with an expectancy of success rather than one of failure?

Failure is and always will be a much easier route to take, but for those of you here, those of you who knew me and what I was about, I hope I've positively influenced you with the expect success attitude.

I leave you with this:

You don't always get what you want and you don't always get what you need. Instead you get what you honestly and truly believe that you deserve. In other words, you get what you expect. So why not expect success?

That right there is my mission. Before we move on, I wish to pose that same question above to you. Answer it openly and honestly. The gates that open to you afterwards are forever rewarding.

John Mulry, MSc

- 5 -

What is Success?

"Successful people are always looking for opportunities to help others. Unsuccessful people are always asking, 'What's in it for me?'"

– Brian Tracy

When I answered Mr. Honan all those years ago saying I want to be successful, my idea of success was much different than it was when I started college, when I came back from a year volunteering in South America, and what it is today.

Too often in today's fast-paced and ever changing world, we are told constantly that we need to do this and we need to do that if we are to be successful.

Success doesn't work like that. Why? Success is individual to the person who craves it or owns it. My idea of success and your idea of success are two completely different things, and rightly so. You could go out and ask 100 people on the street what their idea of success is and I bet you that nearly everyone's answer will differ. Sure, there may be some similarities, but everyone has their own idea of what it is to be successful.

In fact, I did go out and ask people what their idea of success was and I got some very interesting answers back.

The exact question I asked was, "What is success to you?"

Here are some of the answers I got back.

Essentially, John, success must be defined as an internal journey for one's own truth. And that is very counter to the current societal impetus of searching through externally loaded measurements of success that simply line up with contemporary definitions of what that 'means' or 'looks like.' Peeling back the layers of our own egos, conditionings, labels, and judgements in order to answer this single question from the freedom of our own individual nature:

What do you truly want?

Answer that. Then do it.

That's "success."

– Brian Grasso, author of *Audacity of Success*

I had a little think, took some time out, and I've got to be honest... I was actually stumped! Now, to any other person this might seem quite 'normal' (whatever normal is), however to me, it was a proper shocker.

You see, I am a coach... so, to be asked what success is to me and then to be stumped caught me off guard.

The reason is this. I can't give John an answer such as, "To have a squillion quid in the bank account." "To have a flashy car, big house, 20 holidays per year." "To beat your competition." "To love your family." "To achieve your goal." "To survive." "To thrive." "To be happy."

Success is some or all of those things to some people and none of these things to others. So how can we ever truly define 'success' universally?

Answer is, we can't and we likely shouldn't. Success can be and is whatever you or I want it to be.

It's as simple as that. To me personally, I have several things to define my own success. Now, these are personal to me... they are not yours, they are mine; I recommend you explore yours. Here are mine in no particular order, some are measurable and some are not.

To give love. To be loved by someone who actually wants to love me and not just because I 'loved them first.' To be joyful and happy. To live peacefully.

To make 'progress' in anything that I do... I am always happy if I am moving toward something, no matter how slow or fast.

To feel good about myself and to love myself for all of my wonderful imperfections. I have not liked myself in the past and now I do... this is success.

So you see, no cars, cash, or fancy glitzy things here for me.

Success is more of a feeling for me... and I hope it stays that way and I hope my children have similar experiences as they grow and explore their lives.

– Mark Whitehand

"I suppose knowing what you want, getting it, and being able to look back and be satisfied with what you have achieved and be happy and comfortable with that."
– Aidan Whelan

"Success to me is doing something I enjoy, being happy doing it, making enough money to live a happy, healthy lifestyle, and having time to spend with the people who are most important to me."
– Jessica Thompson

"I think success is being fulfilled with who you are and where you are with your life. Where the second-guessing and the, 'I could have or should haves,' are replaced with the, 'I am and I'm doings.'"
– Dawn Arduni Watson

"Ok, so success to me is seeing my business and my personal grow and develop into a well-known brand. I don't measure success from money in the bank, I see creating employment and waking up every morning to what I enjoy as success."
– Kevin Nugent

John Mulry, MSc

"I would say it is both an internal and external measure. Most importantly, internally it is a short-term measure that signals the achievement of current personal goals. It can be a tool to plan your next goals and strive to achieve more. Externally it will be how others perceive your achievements to date based on goals, defined or undefined."
– Kenny Cosgrove

So, what is success for me?

Two years ago when I got pregnant and started to have a family of my own, my whole perspective about success changed. It no longer means earning good money and having shiny work. My hopes and dreams have all boiled down to raising my kid well.

She has to know about Christ. I have to be there for her. God blessed me with a daughter and I carry the responsibility to guide her and raise her properly. So I decided to throw away my traditional work and decided to shift to freelance home-based work with this reason. Why? So I would have time with my family.

Now, I am with my daughter 24/7 and seven days a week. I was there when she learned her first steps, words, and antics. In her little age, I tell her about Jesus. It gives me overwhelming joy whenever she bows down her head to pray and waves her hand in church praise. I am thankful whenever I hear her teacher say she's a very attentive and obedient child. It's hard to be a parent, but I am always thankful I got my child.

Not only this, but given that I am only working at home, I am able to attend to my husband's needs.

I still pray for material things, but those are geared to having financial freedom so my family would live comfortably. To put it simply I guess, success for me is having to balance family life and work.

– Christine Rianne

"I used to think that success was work-related. Now I know that true success is learning to be present in the moment and feeling peaceful in that moment."
– Debbie Gettler

"Any landing I can walk away from."
– Conor O'Sullivan (Airplane Pilot)

"Success for me is to make as much of a positive difference in as many people's lives as possible. If I die knowing I have tried my best to do this, I have achieved success in helping success."
– Michael Smyth

"Success to me is probably gauged on a daily basis; was my day productive? If I can feel content that it was and that I worked my hardest and was true to myself then I would call that success. Not to mention a little bit of muscle twinge, just to prove I pushed the body a little, too, that's the icing on the cake!"
– Cora Molloy

"Success is making the right choices and decisions that lead you to a happier life."
– Dave Walsh

"To say it short: reaching your goals, no matter what, is really success to me."
– Jorgen Anderson

"Success is happiness! Happiness is family, friends, and they all equal unconditional love."
– Ashling Devlin

"Success is the feeling when I know that I have thrown 100% of my mind and body into achieving a goal."
– Brianna Hatswell

"Success can be valued or judged from a vast amount of factors from a person's goals and achievements. What is success? For some:

- *It's getting out of bed each and every day.*
- *It's passing a test.*
- *It's living.*
- *Achieving a fitness goal / target.*
- *Maintaining an achievement.*
- *Making or creating something.*
- *Surviving.*
- *Falling in love.*
- *Enjoying a holiday.*
- *Travelling.*
- *Buying your first car.*
- *Paying off a loan.*
- *Beating an illness.*

The list goes on and for me I suppose I can tick off everything on that list already. The thing with success is that we all achieve it every day without realising it. The goal is to appreciate your success; embrace it, acknowledge it, and allow it to form you into the person you strive to be. Success should equal happiness."

– Stephen Hardiman

"Success for me is living a reflective life where one's focus is more on being than on doing or having."
– Colman Collins

"Success is a very intrinsically founded thing that varies greatly from person to person; providing they truly understand what success is.

"The commonplace and media-hyped fallacy that success is the glamour, the grab at a moment of unauthentic fame, a huge bank balance, and a flashy car are in fact missing the point.

"Success is yours to have in whatever guise it may be to you, but one fundamental underpinning element, you feel happy. Your day, even if average, is one of joy and fulfilment. I aim for this simple yet undeniable success."

Your Elephant's Under Threat

– Peter Walkom

"To me success is peace of mind, keeping balance in my life with awareness to stop and think."
– Sheila Lally

"Success to me is: 1. contentment within my business affairs 2. ensuring that my family is provided for 3. good health and 4. being in the company of good friends."
- Liam Bluett

"Success is a totally honest and loving acceptance of oneself, followed by attainment of challenging goals premised on this acceptance."
– Kevin Newell

"Success is when you set a goal and work as hard as you possibly can and you surpass that goal. When you can look back at what you have achieved and say, 'I really did it!' and really be proud of what you have accomplished."
– Annette Clark

"Success to me is doing the thing you love to do, with the people you love to be with, it's about giving back and achieving the results your heart's desire truly wants in life. It's about living your goals, not someone else's. And ultimately, it's the progressive realisation of your true potential in life."
– Declan Loy

"I told my wife that I was taking on a life coach to help me become a better man. I mentioned that I was asked about what my meaning of success was, and she immediately sent me a quote by David Brinkley, an American broadcast journalist: 'A successful man is one who can lay a firm foundation with the bricks others have thrown at him.'

"I thought about that, and as I continued to ponder my own thoughts on success, I began to realise that success is not really something you 'get' or 'become.' It is not a big bank roll, a fancy car, or a coveted position in a mega firm with a corner office. There are many people with all of that, and in spite of it all, they are still unhappy. Contrarily, there are many more people without any of that, and they live their lives to the fullest. So, who is more successful?

"Success is simply: doing what you can with what you have, to the best of your abilities. If you can look at yourself in the mirror at the end of it and think, 'I've done well,' then you have achieved success. After all, success is a journey in life, not a destination... and if it were not for the journey, we'd already be there."

– Jon McCarty

"I used to believe that success was about monetary wealth and fame. I now believe that success is trying to do the very best one can with the talents one has. Being true to oneself and not influenced by what others think. I believe success comes from within and is about achieving one's potential, about meeting one's goals and having peace of mind."
– Sean Gallagher

As you can see, the commonality amongst the answers is that there is none. Success is truly only defined by the meaning that you yourself give it. I cannot tell you what it is for you, just like no one can tell me what it is for me.

My own definition of success goes something like this....

> Success to me isn't money or material things. It's not holidays, accolades, or recognition. Those things are nice, and yes I crave them, want them, and will get them, but they pale in comparison to what true success is. To me it's twofold:
>
> Firstly, true success is finding, opening up to, and loving someone. Waking up every day beside someone who makes the dullest day shine, someone who drives you to be the best you can be, gives you that spark

when you need it, supports you, and gives you a reason why.

Secondly, success is to constantly learn and grow. To invest in yourself, consume what you invest in, and act upon what you consume. Success is yours once – and only – when you choose to expect it.

A discussion with my sister really drove this point home for me. It was when I was in the midst of my transition from purely fitness to the academy as it is today. In hindsight, it was apparent that I didn't fully and openly communicate to her what my future plans were, and when she aired this to me I snapped.

The reason I snapped was because I was under threat – she was showing concern, which I mistook for judgement. It bothered me for a few days, but talking it over with my coach led me to come to the conclusion that we both had different ideas of what success was.

My idea of success isn't the traditional one. I tried the traditional route of working for someone and earning success through that means, a means that is perfectly acceptable and rewarding. It just wasn't for me. When I told her I was going through some changes in my business, she mistook this as my moving away completely from what I was doing and she feared I was making a mistake. I guess I sensed this and that is why I snapped.

The point here is that we all do have different ideas of what success is, but if we don't openly communicate it with each other then how can we actively try to pursue it? We won't. We'll fall victim to someone else's ideals and start pursuing their goals instead.

Here are some questions that you can answer yourself. Again, please answer them openly and honestly.

- What is success to you?

- How will you know once you've achieved it?
- Who else benefits from your succeeding?
- What have you done today that will bring you closer to it?
- Who do you know or who can you find that has already achieved similar success?
- Who can you enlist to help you achieve it?

Those questions aren't random. They are specific and they follow a creed, one that is worthwhile. The creed we will be discussing in greater detail much later, but for now, here are the key points:

- Your success will come easier if, by the result of your success, others succeed, too. Or you succeed in result of helping others succeed first.
- Your focus must be kept constant; it must be present in your mind at all times.
- The third comes back to the phrase, "If I have seen further, it is because I have stood on the shoulders of giants."

You don't need to go it alone. Specifically, there are three types of people that are best suited to helping you. Note that these three people aren't necessarily friends or family members, either. More on that later.

- 6 -

Change

"If you do what you've always done, you'll get what you've always gotten."

–Tony Robbins

There is absolutely nothing special about me. Zilch. Nada. Zero.

Well, maybe apart from a few crazy things like being born on Friday the 13th, being in jail in Brazil, a crazy shark/surgery encounter, and a hallucinogenic time in the jungle to name a few. For now, these stories can wait. The story I'm sharing with you here is one of change. How I've changed and how you can, too.

Have I completely 'arrived?' Nope. Not completely.

It's a journey, one I'm embracing. I have direction, reason, and I have that happy feeling deep down, knowing that in years to come I'll know I've made the decisions to be the best that I can be, every day.

But it wasn't always like this.

Not by a long shot....

Tony Robbins, someone I think is a force of nature and an incredible person (I have yet to meet him), describes that in order for you to change, you need to experience either inspiration or desperation.

I couldn't agree more. In different periods of my life it was inspiration and desperation that led me to change. I'll be detailing these experiences with you in the hopes that you can draw some inspiration from them.

I'm going to be completely honest with you... some of what I'm about to share with you I have never shared with others (not even close friends or family).

If we were to rewind back just a few short years, you'd see me with no energy, no direction, and definitely no happiness. I didn't have a girlfriend (and was too scared to even approach women).

The question for me was, "How can I be happy, truly happy?"

And the problem was I had no idea how.

Back then, I never really knew how to achieve anything meaningful and, honestly, I was too lazy and too preoccupied to do anything about it.

I was more interested in late night parties and lots of booze. It was my way of coping. I'd drink myself stupid. Practically. While it's a myth that you kill brain cells when you drink, I sure as hell gave it my best shot to prove it was true.

I didn't drink because of peer pressure or because it was the norm (although that didn't help). I drank because I was disgusted by my appearance and because I felt so alone. It was my way out. My way of dealing with things... my escape from reality.

San Diego

Deep down, I knew I wasn't treating my body right; sometimes I'd try to change or get healthier but that would usually end in failure because my late night priorities would take over. I always wanted my ideal body and knew it would lead to better things, yet I never took any meaningful action on it – I thought it just wasn't meant for me.

In the summer of 2007, I went to San Diego, CA, and I think that's when I got my first taste of health and fitness being such a prominent part of everyday life.

I remember my address exactly. We lived (there were eight of us) in a two-bedroom apartment in between the lake and the beach on Mission Boulevard, Mission Beach. There was me, Eunan, Andrew, Paddy, TJ, Niall, Kevin, and James. Talk about a bunch of messers on an extended holiday. It was pretty amazing. That summer I got into seriously strange situations but learned a lot of very valuable life lessons, too.

America might have one of the highest rates of obesity, but on the golden beaches of Pacific and Mission Beaches where I spent the summer, you could see that health and fitness were a priority.

On those beaches you could see that people cared about their appearance. Better still, they actually did something that I felt I couldn't do. They were actively improving. Not just thinking about improving, but actually doing it. They were actively doing something about it. The seed was sown.

Throughout that summer and when I returned home, I continued with the late night partying (I could write a separate book about all the crap I've done, trouble I've been in, and stories to tell), but I also started reading a few fitness and motivational books and I really got into them.

These books started painting a picture:

Maybe I could transform for the better, too?

It wasn't just these books that inspired me to change, though.

John Mulry, MSc

South America – The Year That Changed Everything

"Everything you've ever wanted is on the other side of fear."

–George Addair

You know, I am not the same person I was a few years back, and I mean this from a mental, spiritual, and physical point of view.

Back in 2009 I went through some major changes in my life and my direction.

After college, I eventually came to a crossroads in my life – I wasn't happy in my career/job so I decided to pack it in, take some time out, and figure out what I wanted from my life.

I headed off to South America, where I spent a year volunteering and travelling. A lot happened in that year. Good and bad. Here are some of the highlights and lowlights of that year.

Living with an Ecuadorian family and learning Spanish.

When we first arrived, we wanted to completely immerse ourselves so we got four weeks of Spanish lessons in a school and lived with an amazing Ecuadorian woman and her family. We called her 'mama' because that's essentially what she was. She minded us, cooked for us, and made sure we did our homework.

Climbing a volcano and getting stranded.

One day after Spanish school, we decided we'd climb the volcano overlooking Quito; we didn't realise how quickly it gets dark, though. No equipment, no food or water, and only a keyring torch, we had to climb down from practically the top of Pinchincha volcano in complete darkness. Sliding down the side of a volcano in the dark is fun and frightening.

Getting robbed and being left with essentially nothing.

While travelling to Pisco in Peru to volunteer, my backpack was stolen and I was left with only my wallet, passport, and camera. Everything else was taken. I had just bought a laptop, too. It turned out to be one of the best things to happen, though, as I encountered so much kindness from others who donated so much to me.

Swimming with sharks and having surgery on the same day.

While on the Paradise Islands of the Galapagos, we went swimming with sharks and I slashed my arm on the coral, leaving a gaping hole in my arm – I had to swim a few hundred metres with blood pouring out of me and all types of marine life (turtles, seals, fish, and God knows what else) staring at me. I got picked up by a local then and was brought for surgery with two 'doctors' who had me in stitches (both literally and figuratively). Was told no alcohol, no pork, and not to go in the water for two weeks. All of which I did the next day - cue an infection and an extra week on the islands - totally worth it, though.

Volunteering in the Ecuadorian Jungle.

I spent four weeks in the jungle with some crazy animals, crazier people, and no electricity but lots of fun – it was fantastic. I also discovered the best mosquito repellent known to man – rum, and lots of it!

Swimming with piranha.

They don't attack you - they do, however, taste delicious as we had to catch our dinner and we ate them guys.

Your Elephant's Under Threat

Walking with dinosaurs.

This is actually one of the biggest secrets of South America - you can actually climb into the footprints of actual dinosaurs from God knows how many millions of years ago. For someone who loves them, it was one of the highlights of Bolivia. I also got to see and hold actual fossils of dinosaurs, too. Truly incredible.

Having ayahuasca in the jungle (twice).

If you don't know what it is, here's a definition from Wiki:

> *"People who have consumed ayahuasca report having massive spiritual revelations regarding their purpose on earth, the true nature of the universe, as well as deep insight as how to be the best person they possibly can. This is viewed by many as a spiritual awakening and what's often described as afterbirth. In addition it is often reported that individuals can gain access to higher spiritual dimensions and make contact with various spiritual or extra dimensional beings who can act as guides or healers. It's nearly always said that people experience profound positive changes in their life subsequent to consuming ayahuasca and it is often viewed as one of the most effective tools of enlightenment. However, during an ayahuasca experience, people sometimes report nausea, diarrea, and cold flashes. Additionally, vomiting almost always follows ayahuasca ingestion; this purging is considered by many shamans and experienced users of ayahuasca to be an essential part of the experience as it represents the release of negative energy and emotions built up over the course of one's life. There are many reports of miraculous physical as well as emotional and spiritual healing resulting from the use of ayahuasca."*

I can say without a doubt I experienced all of that and then some. I most certainly wasn't the same after it, that's for sure. I often think about it and wonder if it was one of my turning points in life. What I experienced during the ceremony was eye-opening and uplifting. I can remember every detail of that night.

The core theme of my ayahuasca experience was one of reaching and loneliness. Here's what happened. After the shaman brought us through the ceremony, we were brought by boat (we were staying in the middle of the Amazon Jungle just outside of Iquitos) back to where our guide lived. We were sleeping outside in hammocks covered with mosquito nets.

All that night my experience was one of flashbacks, flash forwards, and a present reality that all was not right. I had many episodes that night; in each of them I was always reaching for something but never quite able to grab hold of it. This was symbolic because all my life up until this point I was reaching out for things I thought I wanted.

I was pursuing goals that were never mine, going after things I didn't really care for, always reaching, never grabbing.

The other theme hit home hard. That night I had many adventures; we all did. I was under the impression that we all went off together. We didn't. I left everyone that night and went off on my own. I was under the impression that everyone – Steve, Proinnsias, Isabella, and Martin – was with me. They weren't. I was alone all night and in reality I was alone in life.

Sure I had friends – close friends – family, and loved ones. I felt alone, I felt isolated, and I knew change was coming. The next day, we all discussed our experiences with each other and agreed that something had happened; we all felt different.

That experience, and it's one I admit I don't fully understand, had a profound effect on me. Because since that night, I never felt like I was reaching for anything again. From that day I knew that the path I was on was my own and I don't have to reach. I was expecting to get what I wanted so I didn't have to.

This story I have not shared with anyone but my closest friends.

The next few things actually happened in the space of about five days.

Thrown in Jail in Rio de Janeiro.

We got arrested, thrown in jail, and got beaten up repeatedly for something we didn't even do. I was put on the phone with a fake Irish embassy member and then got beaten again. The local police were as corrupt as you get – I was then threatened with deportation and was brought to the federal police (who thankfully were not corrupt). They realised what happened and sorted everything out, but we were told we had to leave Brazil in six days or less.

This situation led me to drastically rethink my priorities and really drove a stake in between me and alcohol. I've had many (probably too many) run-ins because of alcohol and I've had more blackouts than I can remember (oxymoron?) but this one really hit home for me.

I was always reliant on alcohol. I couldn't go out without drinking. I couldn't work up the courage to talk to girls without 'Dutch courage.' This had to stop. It was getting me nowhere in a hurry. I used to blame my nationality. I'm Irish, we're supposed to be drunks. Total cop out.

Something had to change here. Alcohol was controlling my life and it wasn't a very good driver. Ever since that night in the cell I've had a certain disdain for alcohol and, from then on, I seriously curbed my drinking habits. Don't get me wrong, I still drink and I've had a few slip ups since that night, but after what happened, my love story with alcohol was well and truly over.

Getting kidnapped in Rio de Janeiro.

Well kind of - the world cup was on and we were on Coco Cabaña Beach watching Germany play Spain. We met some Brazilians and went back to their place. We didn't realise they lived in the poverty-stricken favellas of Rio. They didn't want us to leave and even brought us toothbrushes so we'd stay and party with their families. We eventually got away by promising them we'd come back. We didn't.

Getting rescued by helicopter.

While jumping about in the water on the beach in Rio, I was swept out by some sudden waves and couldn't get back in. A surfer came over (that's how far out I was swept) and gave me his surf board while I waited for the lifeguards. They came but the waves were so strong they couldn't bring me in. So further out we went, away from the waves – and around 40 minutes later, a helicopter came and scooped me out with a massive net, like a big fish. I was dropped on the beach in front of a gathering of a couple hundred onlookers. It took me four years to get back in the water.

Falling in love with the people and town of Pisco.

I was meant to stay two weeks and ended up staying for 14 (the first time). The people, the town, and the other volunteers have helped shape me into the person I am - I'll forever be grateful to that little town of Pisco.

They are all pretty amazing, shocking, and strange things that happened, I know, but I wanted to share them with you for a reason. Our past experiences help shape who we are whether we like it or not. They don't define us but they do help shape us. Later on in the book I'll be discussing just why embracing the past and sharing it with others is one of the best things you can do.

– 8 –

Hardship

"Challenges are what make life interesting and overcoming them is what makes life meaningful."

–Joshua J. Marine

You might say that I'm 'lucky' that I have what I have now. I'm actually not a believer in luck, to be honest. I believe that our choices in life really do define who we are and who we become.

Being in a position where I can be proud of myself, my business, my direction, my body, and my bundles of energy is great – but it wasn't until I experienced true hardship that I realised just how lucky I am.

The most influential thing that happened to me was my time volunteering in Peru. To say it was a life-changing experience is an understatement. The volunteer work I did, especially the earthquake relief work in Pisco, was an amazing and enriching experience I'll never forget.

I'll be forever grateful for my time there as it made me realise one of my true passions – helping others. I remember the day I left, I cried on the bus – it was an accumulation of 11 months of emotion, but I was happy because I had helped so many people change their lives. But I also realised that, over those 11 months, I'd changed my own life, too.

The biggest thing I learned all through my time in South America is how the people there deal with their lives and their situations.

I met and became close friends with some of the nicest, most humbling people in the world; they were also the happiest people I have ever met in my life. And do you know what else? They were also the same group of people who had encountered the most hardship I have ever come across.

How can people who have encountered so much hardship be so happy?

I know, I couldn't figure it out either. They had every right to be the most bitter, angriest people in the world, but they weren't. They truly loved life and were thankful every single day for being alive.

Proinnsias (my friend I was travelling with) and I got really close with one person in particular while we were in Pisco volunteering.

As I mentioned we only intended to stay two weeks but ended up staying 14 the first time we were there (I later went back before returning to surprise my mam while she was 'shopping' in New York).

His name was Martin, and I now consider him a brother. He went through so much and suffered so much hardship (like so many others in Pisco), yet when he walked into a room his smile lit the whole place up.

He didn't place any great importance on fancy things, gizmos, or gadgets. The most important thing to him was friendship and a sense of belonging.

This stayed with me and I've always wanted to emulate this feeling in my everyday life, when interacting with people, and when I'm with my coaching clients.

I guess one of the first lessons for you here is, no matter how hard you think it is, no matter how much you suffered in the past, you can come out the other side and you can *choose* to do it while feeling sorry for yourself, or you can *choose* to do it with a smile on your face and be thankful for all the amazing things you have going for you.

Your Elephant's Under Threat

It's your life experience that shapes you into the person you are; it's your bad times as well as your good times. When you learn how to choose to focus on the positive, you'll be like Martin, the person that lights up a room when they walk into it.

John Mulry, MSc

- 9 -

Dad

"It is never too late to be what you might have been."

–George Eliot

It took me a long while before my experiences from South America began to sink in and take shape. You see, there was another source of change for me that was more desperation than inspiration, and that was my father. Unfortunately, through my father, I got to see the effects of not looking after yourself.

My father's health deteriorated so much over the last few years. This was a big shock to my system and crushed my beliefs. Growing up he was always the biggest, strongest person I knew. My friends were in awe of him – 6 foot 6 inches tall and strong as you like. I remember in school we used to have arguments about whose father would 'kill' whom. When anyone saw my dad they'd immediately shut up. He was a giant of man. And he, too, shaped me into who I am.

He worked so hard to provide for us, he always strived to give us everything, and he sacrificed a lot. He gave up everything for me, my sister, and my mother, and to be honest, I never fully appreciated it. Because he worked so much, we never really built up a typical father-son relationship. I was always a lot closer to my mam.

He never had as much time to play with me as a kid as he would have liked and I think that hurt him.

He also had lots of health problems, many of which came down to him not taking care of his body and his exercise, and his nutrition was not as good as it should have been. He spent the last decade or so in and out of hospitals and I saw first-hand the effects it had on him but also the effects it had on us, his loved ones. Sadly, he passed away in January of 2013.

However, I can thank him for his help in shaping me into the person I am today and I promised him, my mother, and myself I would not let others suffer the way he did.

It was my father's deteriorating health and my time in San Diego and South America that led me to a decision. A decision I didn't take lightly. I knew I was going to change. I had to. You have to remember I kept all of this hardship bottled up and didn't tell anyone.

Maybe you're in a similar position now. With the pathways I'll be discussing later in the book, I'll give you the tools and systems so you can arrive at the decision to change much quicker than I did and hopefully with much less hardship.

I was stuck in a rut and couldn't see any way out. I hated my job. Before I launched the Expect Success Academy, I worked in corporate finance. I had it to a point where I completely automated work through excel macros. In fact, I spent roughly 10% of my working day actually working and the rest seeking a way out. Not unlike the rest of the corporate world, I guess.

I sought solace in bottles of vodka and junk food on the weekends (and weekdays if I could get away with it).

On paper, I was successful: graduated with honours, Masters under the belt, got a secure job, heading in the 'right direction'....

The thing is, I didn't *feel* successful. In fact, I was pretty miserable. I felt slow, lethargic, and lost. I kept it bottled up, though. I didn't tell anyone. Life was pretty crappy.

All I wanted was to feel proud about the way I looked and have the confidence and energy to do the things I enjoy. Be able to do the things I knew I should be doing. Live a life I could be proud of. I wanted to be able to feel confident about my physique. I wanted to be noticed. The problem was I had no idea how. The problem was I was falling for everything and succeeding at nothing. It was like a weird fetish I had when I was younger.

John Mulry, MSc

– 10 –

Fitness and Fetishes

"In order to succeed, your desire for success should be greater than your fear of failure."

–Bill Cosby

Growing up wasn't easy for me. In school, I was bullied; I had friends, don't get me wrong, but I was always an easy target because I'm naturally an introvert.

There was this one guy... he bullied me, called me names, and made me feel awful. He hated me for some reason. He hated a lot of people. In fact, he hated himself, too, because years later he committed suicide.

When I was younger, I had a problem with my ears... well, let's just say that my head hadn't quite grown into my ears yet, so I was teased a lot. My confidence took a beating because of this, so when I was younger I was never any good at acting on my wants or desires.

Actually, looking back, maybe that teasing and bullying spurred me on to want to change so badly.

I had a bit of a 'fetish' when I was younger. I'd stay up late. I would wait until everyone in my house had gone to bed. I'd close my sitting room door and put on the television.

Volume would be down real low so I wouldn't wake anyone.

Then I started watching...

late night...

infomercials....

I would watch all the fitness equipment infomercials. I had an addiction or fetish for watching them... I'd stay up until all hours looking at them. As much as I enjoyed watching the ladies in their scantily clad gym wear, that wasn't the reason. I was addicted to looking for the easy way out. The easy way to achieve my dream body.

I took it a step further, though.

Andre Chaperon asked me a question once:

If you had two choices, the easy (quick) option or the harder (slower) option, which would you choose?

Sadly, I always used to choose the easy way out. Take my late night fetish as an example. Have you seen those commercials? Sadly, it's this type of easy, quick fix/hype stuff that sells. It's sexy and irresistible. And sadly, sexy and irresistible sells.

I was the biggest sucker of them all.

Not only did I stay up late in the hopes I'd find some magic bullet, I'd also actually *bought* the damn things. Not just one. Two. Three or four. I bought tonnes. My bedroom was full of the junk.

Did I get results? Nope. What did I get? Well, apart from a lot of glorified clothes hangers and some real strange and downright nonsensical advice (one that was so weird I wore a hat every time I worked out because I thought I'd get a six pack quicker), I got more frustrated and felt like I was never going to be able to be physically proud.

Now, the only reason I'm telling you this (rather embarrassing) story is to demonstrate a couple of important points.

A lot of what is out there is pure bullshit. Sexy, *irresistible* nonsense. And that goes for everything. Not just fitness-related stuff. Business-related, self-help, and personal development are included.

And it sells like hot cakes.

I've bought into all the hype and hoopla and maybe you have at some point, too. It feels pretty demoralising to buy into something only for it to let you down, doesn't it?

On the other hand, there *are* solutions out there that are valuable, effective, and will help you succeed. There are solutions out there where the focus is on adding value, building relationships, and personal growth for you.

How you find those solutions and how they find you is different for everyone.

Everyone's path is different... please remember that. My path of continuous failure, mistakes, making some fantastic discoveries, going on some crazy adventures, and more failures led me to writing this book and your path, no matter what it has been, has led you to reading it.

Fitness

When I started out on my path of change (which was initially one of health and fitness), I knew that I had to find out more about exercise and nutrition. No-brainer, right?

Back then there was no internet and no computers (my first computer was a Commodore 64 - I loved that thing), so the only way to get information was from fitness magazines.

Problem. Big problem. Because I was naturally shy and my self-confidence was constantly taking a beating, I was way too scared to buy these magazines in the fear of being judged by anyone and everyone that saw me with them.

So I didn't buy any of them. Ever. When I first started out, I can honestly say I never bought a fitness magazine. Turns out this was a good thing. A very, *very* good thing. This in turn meant I was never subjected to the barrage of information, conflicting advice, and mixed messages that were out there.

Is that all they are? No, of course not, but they are very confusing, and when you're a beginner it can be overwhelming to try to decipher where to start, who to listen to, and what to do.

And when it comes to change in other areas, it can be even worse. There are even more voices in the crowd. Shouting. Screaming at you to, "do this," or, "do that."

We're constantly being bombarded left, right, and centre with marketing messages and social media updates. Everything is happening so fast. Just when you think you've learned something, it's outdated. Our smart phones and email messages seem to rule us and if you're not on the 500 different social media sites, you're a failure.

And that's just the technology and business side of things.

When you introduce our personal lives and health issues into the mix, it becomes nigh on impossible to find the time to figure out the things you really want.

Is it any wonder you don't know where to turn? Don't know where to start? Don't know who to listen to?

It can be an absolute maze out there. The mixed messages leave you lost and alone.

You're doing something you think is right, then you're told what you're doing is wrong and you're useless. How the heck can you win? You can't. I know because I was a loser, just like you.

- 11 -

Loser

"I have been impressed with the urgency of doing. Knowing is not enough; we must apply. Being willing is not enough; we must do."

–Leonardo da Vinci

I was confused. I didn't know where to start. I didn't know who to trust. I didn't know what I should be doing.

I was lost, alone, depressed, a borderline alcoholic, directionless, uninspired, disgusted about my appearance, and completely confused about all the mixed messages in life, relationships, and business. I was clueless about what I was supposed to do, who I was supposed to be, where I was supposed to start, and I couldn't see a way out. Basically, I was a loser.

I don't mean loser as a derogatory term. What I mean is, I was like you in that I was playing the game of life in a way I couldn't win, and hence, I was losing.

There were (and still are) so many mixed messages and conflicting information. Trying to decipher the substance from the noise and nonsense was completely *overwhelming*! For me, it seemed like trying to find a needle in a haystack. Except worse. A lot worse. The more I read, the more unanswered questions I had.

I was suffering from paralysis of analysis.

> **Analysis paralysis** or **paralysis of analysis** is the state of over-analyzing (or over-thinking) a situation so that a decision or action is never taken, in effect paralyzing the outcome. A decision can be treated as over-

complicated, with too many detailed options, so that a choice is never made, rather than try something and change if a major problem arises. A person might be seeking the optimal or "perfect" solution upfront, and fear making any decision which could lead to erroneous results, when on the way to a better solution.

(Definition from Wikipedia.)

It was almost by mistake that I finally figured it out. To be honest, I didn't realise the process I was actually going through until much later. What I'm saying is I fumbled into succeeding at first.

One of the very first things I started focusing on came from a quote by Sir Isaac Newton.

"If I have seen further, it's because I have stood on the shoulders of giants."

In reading that, I immediately said, "If I'm going to start getting results, I need to find some of my own giants."

As I said, I started studying fitness, nutrition, and especially personal development to almost an obsessive level. My first giant was Tom Venuto. As I mentioned earlier, I studied Tom's work to almost an obsessive level. I didn't pay any attention to anything or anyone else in the beginning.

This is a very important lesson, too. There's tonnes of information out there. Later on in the book I'll be discussing why this is both a good thing and a bad thing, but for now, know this: I attribute a large percentage of my results to the fact that I only listened to one person and followed exactly what they said. What that did was give me consistency.

After I went through the process of transforming myself, I noticed I was getting a lot of questions, especially in the gym. Random people would stop me to ask me questions and my friends were asking me about my changes (what I was doing, eating, etc.). Heck, even professional rugby players visited my gym one time and stopped me to ask about my training methods, and another time WWE wrestlers were in my same gym and they stopped to look at what I was doing and how I was training.

Little did they know that my results had very little to do with my training or the nutritional principles I was following.

John Mulry, MSc

- 12 -

Expect Success

"Limitations live only in our minds. But if we use our imaginations, our possibilities become limitless."

–Jamie Paolinetti

I loved helping others when they'd ask – it brought me back to my time in Peru. I had changed so much for the better because of health and fitness and now I was getting the opportunity to help others change, too… that's when I had a revelation.

My *Aha!* moment – what if I could combine my passion for helping people and my passion for health and fitness?

So I switched careers. Some of my friends and family were shocked – others were delighted because they could see I was following my true passion. Expect Success Fitness was born.

I immerse myself in study, to learn, and dissect every fitness and business book I could while also studying for my certifications – all this while still working full time, continuing my own training, and training some friends and family whenever I could.

There were endless nights of study and early mornings, lots of missed events, gigs, and get-togethers, but I didn't care because I was following my dream. I set myself the goal of moving back home and starting Expect Success Fitness.

Funnily, one of the first things I did was fly halfway across the world to California to learn from the best of the best when it comes to fitness. I got to hang out with bodybuilding legend Ronnie Coleman and learn from fitness business expert Bedros Keulian.

These encounters pushed me further out of my comfort zone. When I got back I invested (a lot lof money) in coaching from world renowned fitness expert and business coach Cabel McElderry... and he coached me through the process of starting my business.

Back in Galway, I secured rights to train out of the exclusive spa and health club at one of the most prestigious hotels in Ireland, The Meyrick, and all the magic began. Clients started coming in and they started getting amazing results.

I started writing for one of my local papers, which is how I met Jess – best day of my life.

I continued going to courses, events, and seminars and flew to London, where I studied at Birmingham University and was mentored by experts such as Jon le Tocq, Brian Grasso, Nick Nanton, and Dax Moy. I even went to Texas to continue my learning and studied under Dan Kennedy and GKIC marketing experts Darcy Juarez and Dave Dee so I could improve myself and thus improve my clients' results.

The decision to go to Texas started a rollercoaster ride I never imagine and set in motion events that are now coming full circle. Going to Texas solidified my belief in and the power of direct response marketing, which now is a cornerstone of the Expect Success Academy. It also set forth the actions that led me to being hand picked and trained by Dan Kennedy and GKIC, to become their main man here in Ireland.

As I said, I consider myself a hunter of success and will take any suitable opportunity to further myself and my clients.

– 13 –

I Was Part of the Problem

"Expose yourself to your deepest fear; after that, fear has no power, and the fear of freedom shrinks and vanishes. You are free."

–Jim Morrison

The thing is – and I may just be the first expert to ever admit this to you – but it wasn't all rosy... not all of my clients got amazing results. The majority did, but there were some who just didn't.

Back then I thought it was their fault, that they just weren't cut out for my style of training and that they obviously didn't want it bad enough. I was wrong... dead wrong.

Bucket

The problem of achieving your goals has nothing to do with your genes, time, money, ability, skill level, or the fact that you're maybe too lazy, too slow, or anything like that. The problem starts with the simple analogy of a bucket.

You're probably thinking, *a bucket?* Bear with me.

Think of your life as a bucket... a blue one. I like the colour blue.

This bucket gets filled with all of the 'stuff' happening in your life: work, home, spouse, kids, social life, play, weekends, friends, partying, bills, problems, eating right, exercising, worrying about the future, the past, and the present, stress, money... everything.

All this stuff fills up your bucket, and what happens if you have a full bucket? It tips over. You crash, you cave, you can't cope, you fail (at something), you can't start anything, and you can't change.

Now all of these seemingly minor things that fill your bucket are threats... to you, your life, your happiness, and your ability to succeed. I'll be discussing these threats and how we go about emptying your bucket in the following pages.

It wasn't until I started getting help, coaching and masterminding, and completed a course from a superstar called Dax Moy that I realised that it wasn't my clients' fault they didn't get results... it was mine. Even though I didn't know it at the time, I was hindering their progress, not helping them.

I realised that I needed to seriously shift the way I do things if I was going to fulfil my mission of instilling the expect success attitude in others and becoming the catalyst for their success.

I used to be one of the shouters. Not anymore. The whole concept of everyone shouting at you and confusing you doesn't sit well with me and it doesn't do anything for your results. What if we 'experts' were to work together in harmony to help you?

Now that would be something worth shouting about, right? If I only I'd known that back then.

My clients not getting the best results possible wasn't because I was bad at what I did or because they weren't committed enough. It was because their bucket was too full.

I was filling their bucket even more when I should have been emptying it. I was being a major threat to them: not helping, but hindering.

Threat

If you're currently unhappy with your business or the direction you're heading, I'm going to hypothesise that you're currently

Your Elephant's Under Threat

losing and you're feeling confused, unfocused, distracted, directionless, uninspired, tired, stressed, alone, slow, unmotivated, isolated, sad, angry, bored, and lost.

Essentially, you're feeling *threatened*.

Being under threat is the #1 reason holding you back from achieving the life, the business, the body, the confidence, and the energy you want and need.

Please re-read that sentence again. The reason you cannot change, even though you know you have to, is because you're under threat.

When you 'get' this, everything changes. And it's a simple process to work through. Don't worry – we'll be going through that exact process in this book.

When I figured this out, I had an epiphany... a massive brainwave: If I was going to succeed in my mission of instilling the "Expect Success" attitude into people under threat and struggling, then things had to change. I had to change. My business and business model had to change.

I also discovered (through a coaching session with fantastic coach Mark Whitehand) that one of the threats I had in my life was that I was seeking the recognition and approval of my father, who had passed away in January. The threat was the fact that I was seeking my father's approval and couldn't fully move forward until I addressed that. It was a massive boulder in front of me, one which I couldn't see.

I don't think he fully grasped why I left my 'secure job' when I did to start my own business. I felt I was always seeking his approval and striving to make him proud.

Remember, I never really communicated to anyone that I was miserable. On the outside, I was 'happy.' I kept my depression, confusion, and unhappiness bottled in... I guess it was understandable if he didn't grasp the idea.

What I came to realise was that my father never worried about my decision… he was worried about whether or not I was happy.

Mark asked me, "Are you happy now?"

I said, "Yes…."

Then Mark said, "Then your dad is happy, too. And he was always proud of you."

I'll never forget that moment because I broke down, and actually reliving it and typing it here for you has caused me to again. Thank you, Mark, and thank you so much for everything, Dad.

When that threat was lifted, everything was so much clearer… I knew what I wanted to do and could see the path clearly.

When I came back from that session, I decided to go back to the drawing board.

With the help of some of my best clients – Liam, Kevin, Kenny, Seamus, Sean, Ben, and Stephen – and one of my coaches, David, I decided that if I was going to succeed in my mission, then Expect Success Fitness (as it was) had to die.

Some of my best clients were successful business professionals and self-employed men. They went from overweight, depressed, and unhappy to being proud of their bodies, having more energy, and enjoying life again.

They were well-equipped to pass on their knowledge and expertise, and thankfully, were happy to do so.

From the ashes of Expect Success Fitness has risen the Expect Success Academy, where the core focus is on being a catalyst for your change so you can succeed in business and in life.

– 14 –

Four Important Points

"Dream big and dare to fail."

–Norman Vaughan

The reason I wanted to share my story with you is to illustrate four important points:

- We all face adversity
- Opportunity is everywhere
- Success isn't linear
- Change is good

Through telling you my story I wanted to show you that I am just an ordinary guy who's made a lot of mistakes but come out the other side expecting success instead of failure. I'm ordinary, but I strive for the extraordinary.

Adversity

Everyone, no matter what your age, gender, race, status, or background, has faced and will face adversity. When you start to overcome your threats, chances are you'll come up against adversity. Adversity is like a challenge. A roadblock, testing you, questioning your desire. Adversity, to me, is a way that we can examine how badly we want something.

If you look up the definition of adversity, you can see it has two words associated with it: *state* and *event*.

It's short-term, it's a temporary state or an event in your life, and it doesn't define your life. Just like failure. When you fail at something you are not a failure, you merely failed at that attempt. You found a way that didn't work. That doesn't make you a failure. Choosing to *give up* when you face adversity makes you a failure.

Failure is a choice, not a label. Adversity and failure are intertwined, but so are the many seeds of opportunity that come from adversity and failing.

Seeds of Opportunity

Did you know that the guy who invented Post-It notes failed miserably? When he was inventing the glue that is now used on Post-It notes, his goal was to invent a glue that would stick permanently. He failed at this attempt, but through the seeds of opportunity that were awarded to him for acting, he invented one of most-used (and lucrative) pieces of stationery in history.

He looked for the seeds of opportunity instead of seeing himself as a failure. You can do the same in your life. I'm not going to pretend that everything is going to be all rosy in your life when you go through the Define, Refine, and Align system. It's not, and it's not meant to be.

Adversity and failures have their rightful place in everyone's life. Napoleon Hill said, "Every adversity, every failure, and every heartache carries with it the seed of an equal or greater benefit." This sums it up beautifully. By striving and moving forward, you will be presented with opportunities even when you come up short. Being in a position to recognise these opportunities is key.

The beauty of the Define, Refine, and Align system is that it makes it easier for you to recognise these seeds of opportunity and therefore makes it easier to act upon them.

Success isn't Linear

This book is about change, which I'll discuss in a second, but more than that it's about recognising and accepting yourself. We all have past mistakes and failures, but these past adversities do not define us. Our future is not determined by our past. Our future is determined by recognising our past as part of the journey, whether that past is failed attempts or successful attempts.

This book is about helping you become strong. In order to be strong in every area of your life, you need to recognise your weaknesses and shortcomings for what they are. Not defining moments; they were merely moments. Through recognising that we have past failures and weaknesses that we need to let go, we become truly strong. When we're strong, we can achieve anything. Live the life we want, have a business we love and one that serves us (and others), and have the health and happiness we deserve.

In his fantastic and highly recommended book *Psycho-Cybernetics*, Dr. Maxwell Maltz talks about the need to focus on addressing the now. We cannot change the past, we can only focus on the now. By doing so with a definitive plan, we can have a positive outcome in the future. Your past is important, but do not let yourself be limited by it. Your ability to change your life and your business extends far beyond anything that has happened in your past. That's a 'writer downer' if ever there was one.

Change

The fourth reason I shared my story is to illustrate the point on change. Change is good. I have gone through so much change in my life, some expected, some unexpected. So have you.

All change comes from one thing and one thing alone: action. We will cover how you can determine your own unique action steps in the refine stage. Here's an overview.

Action boils down to doing something you weren't doing already, and when we boil it down, that is what? Change. Doing something you weren't doing already (or you were but doing badly), when you break it down, is change. For example, developing your business/marketing strategy or starting to exercise if you currently live a sedentary lifestyle. Now I know some of you may be thinking, "Change? No, change is bad, can't change. Only bad things happen when you change."

Sorry to burst your bubble, but CHANGE IS GOOD!

- Change helps you to be flexible.
- When you change, you discover new things – new possibilities that weren't there before.
- Change makes you smarter – when you change you learn new things. If you never change, you'll stay stagnant and never learn and grow.
- Change reminds us that anything's possible. When you make positive changes, you can achieve anything.

Nothing stays the same forever; the only thing that is constant is change. You're not the same person you were five years ago, just as you won't be the same five years from now.

Apple

I used to be anti-Apple. I don't even know why, to be honest. Nowadays I love Apple; I love their products, their business, their strategy, and their story. When I finally decide to give up on my Windows laptop, I'll be getting a Mac, no question about it. Now, where you lie on the Apple/Windows divide is irrelevant; what is relevant is that, by changing, I am now able to benefit from the quality of Apple's products, which I couldn't have before. Change is good. Stop. Read that sentence again. *Change is good.*

How can change help you? Well, are you willing to accept that you have to make changes if you want to achieve your goals? If you are, great! If you're not willing to change, is there a reason why? Maybe you think you're not able to change, maybe you think there's just too many things you have to change, or maybe you just don't want to. That's fine, too, by the way – I'm not here to help you if you don't want it. At the end of the day, if you're happy the way you are, I'm happy for you; if you're not, then let's make some changes so you will be.

Your Elephant's Under Threat

Me? Change?

Now you might be thinking, "Yeah sure, John, I know I've got to change but I'm not able to." From a business perspective you might say, "I've tried all the business strategies, I've tried direct mail, online marketing, it's no use." Or in terms of your health you might say, "I've tried all the diets, I tried doing the programs on the TV and workouts in the magazines, I've tried all those things but it's no use, I know change is good but change is hard and SCARY!"

And you're partially right, change is hard and scary, but as we go through the Define, Refine, and Align system together, you'll discover that, while change may be scary, it's also exciting, uplifting, energising, inspiring, and not as hard as you first thought.

When you break change down into something you're confident you can do, it isn't hard. Change is easy. It's still scary, but it's a manageable scary, a scary you have control over. Think for a second. Look at where you are now in your life, your business, or your fitness.

Look at what you've achieved. Now think back to yourself five years ago and where you were then. What aspects of your life have changed? How far have you come? Now think five years into the future and where you'd like to be. The one thing we all want to be in the future is happy, right? I mean no one hopes to be miserable in the future, do they?

Isn't it realistic to think that, just like you change your phone/car/house for a newer improved model, you'll have to change some aspects of your life so you can be a newer, improved, happier, healthier version of yourself in the future?

It's Not Your Fault

The problem is people try to change too many things at once and don't know what to focus on first. This is because there's too much noise out there, too much shit getting shoved down your throat, and you start changing everything at once – or worse, you don't change anything because you don't know where to start. It becomes too much and you quit, dismiss change, and do nothing. Sound familiar?

This happens with anything in life: you get overwhelmed. Too many chores, too many bills, too many projects, too much work – any of these can easily become overwhelming if you try to focus on it all at once. This is where breaking things down into steps helps. Think of it this way, if you have 20 loads of laundry to do and you look at the mountain of it and think about folding and putting away all of it at once, you probably won't end up doing any of it (or maybe one or two loads) because you feel overwhelmed.

Being bombarded with too much at once of anything can be harmful to your progress, which is why staying focused on one thing at a time is so important.

The Solution

What if you had a solution that you could turn to that would outline exactly what to do to make the changes you need to in order to achieve your goals? What if you were given an action plan that you could easily implement that doesn't involve any unnecessary fluff and false promises? What if these changes could be made at a pace you were comfortable with, one you and your success dictates, and with a built-in support and accountability structure?

Well, you have it, and it's in your hands. This book is that action plan.

– 15 –

Long-Term Versus Short-Term

"Do what you can, where you are, with what you have."

–Teddy Roosevelt

The truth is, achieving your goals is built on a set of core principles and frameworks. In this book, I'm giving you those principles and frameworks.

Before we get into the actual systems for overcoming your threats and implementing positive change, you need to be aware of some specific roadblocks that are holding you back. These are the roadblocks that held me back, and they are the same ones that hold back so many others, too.

These roadblocks are:

- Short-term mentality
- Goal hijacking
- Your self-image
- Negative influences

Short-Term Mentality

The short-term mentality (versus the long-term mentality) is a vicious cycle that will hold you back from your full potential and will cause you more harm than good.

It all starts with having a flawed mindset and brainset (see diagram 1). I say brainset because, as you'll discover, when we discuss the topic of our brain's function, makeup, and hormonal activity in depth, mindset's role in our success is often dwarfed by our brain's role.

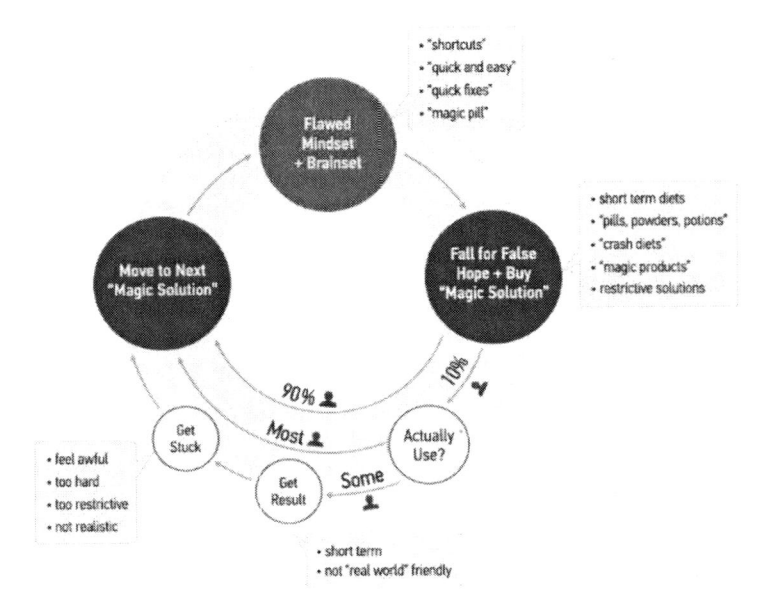

[Diagram: Cycle showing "Flawed Mindset + Brainset" → "Fall for False Hope + Buy 'Magic Solution'" → "Move to Next 'Magic Solution'" with associated labels:
- Flawed Mindset + Brainset: "shortcuts", "quick and easy", "quick fixes", "magic pill"
- Fall for False Hope + Buy "Magic Solution": short term diets, "pills, powders, potions", "crash diets", "magic products", restrictive solutions
- 90% Most Get Stuck: feel awful, too hard, too restrictive, not realistic
- 10% Actually Use? Some Get Result: short term, not "real world" friendly]

Remember I mentioned you were threatened? This is linked, and I'll cover that very soon.

This element is another area of self-help books that is often left out. It puts the whole 'think positive' attitude into perspective and sheds some interesting light on a heavily debated topic.

While I luckily figured this out myself (a very time-consuming, frustrating, and expensive mistake), it wasn't until I wanted to actually be able to communicate and improve my business that I fully comprehended how powerful recognising it was.

I first came across a system similar to this when I completed one of the best email marketing courses I've ever seen by a guy called Andre Chaperon. Andre's a genius at explaining concepts like these. Originally I learned it from him and have adapted it slightly to suit my methods.

The focus of the flawed mindset and brainset is on:

- Shortcuts

Your Elephant's Under Threat

- Quick fixes
- Easy ways out
- 'Magic' solutions

You're always on the lookout for a shortcut to success, a quick fix, an overnight, push-button, done-for-you solution. These are the quick fix, magic bullet solutions and promises of overnight success.

For example, in your business you fall for a hyped up solution that promises to boost sales by 1000% without spending any money or doing any work.

Or in terms of health, the magic exercises, pills, powders, and lotions, or the secret berry from the Amazon Jungle that melts fat. Or the magic pill that guarantees to turn you into a fitness model with no dieting or exercise.

Obviously these examples are a little exaggerated, but you get the point. The next stage of the short-term cycle comes for you after you fall for the hype.

You fall for the hype and the hoopla and buy the "magic beans" in the hope that it'll end your woe and give you everything you want.

Now after you buy into the shortcuts, quick fixes, and easy-way-out solutions, 90% of the time *you don't even use them*. You do nothing. If it's a book, it sits on your shelf or on your hard drive. You never read it, consume it, or apply it. Same goes for software, or a piece of equipment, or a pill, powder, or potion. 90% of the time they don't get used. Whether that's down to you not having time or deep down not fully trusting it to give it proper time and focus, I'm not sure.

You start to feel angry, even more frustrated, alone, and depressed, but lo and behold, another bright and shiny object comes your way. The cycle continues.

Now, out of the 10% that actually use the "quick fix solutions," you might achieve some results, but chances are they are going to be short-lived.

You'll get some results. You might even make a bit of money (if it's business-related) or lose some weight, feel a bit better... but what you're doing isn't long-term.

It isn't sustainable, and when a roadblock comes along, you won't be able to deal with it. The first sign of frustration or feeling stuck and you'll end up right back at the start, falling for the next magic solution or shiny object.

Because what you were doing was too hard, too confusing, too embarrassing, too restrictive, sometimes even illegal, or not fit for the "real world" or for real people with real lives and real commitments.

Does this make sense?

The sooner you realise that the above cycle is seriously flawed, the sooner you can go on to actually start achieving your goals.

Take a second to think about whether or not you're in or have been in a cycle similar to the short-term flawed cycle. It can be completely draining, depressing, and expensive, can't it?

When you start to gravitate towards the long-term cycle, you'll forget about the shiny objects very quickly and the flawed mindset/brainset cycle becomes a distant memory.

Goal Hijacking

This is somewhat related to the short-term cycle. The topic of goal hijacking is something that I didn't fully grasp until I interviewed nutritional expert Brad Pilon. After talking with Brad, it became clear to me that this process is actually commonplace in every area of our lives.

Your Elephant's Under Threat

Goal hijacking is basically allowing yourself (or your business) to be influenced by outsiders. You start with one goal in mind but, after discussing or meeting with people, whether they are your friends, family, peers, or even experts, your goal gets hijacked and you end up with a goal you *think* you should follow because they tell you to.

The best way to describe goal hijacking is with a story.

I've mentioned that I go to a lot of seminars and courses to better myself and my business. The great thing about these is you get to surround yourself with like-minded people.

One of the drawbacks is that goal hijacking is rife at these types of events.

When I first started Expect Success Fitness (before it became the Expect Success Academy), it was never my goal to start a bootcamp or fitness classes. I wanted to train professionals one on one. That was my goal.

When I went to these seminars or courses, all I heard was, "You need a bootcamp. You have to be doing a bootcamp and fitness classes with groups of 20 or more if you want to be successful."

Even my sister was telling me I should be doing classes and I need to start a bootcamp. The thing is, I didn't want to do classes and I didn't want to start a bootcamp.

What I wanted didn't matter because I started doubting what I *was* doing because everyone else was telling me I *should* be doing something else. Everyone was telling me that the only way to succeed was to do a bootcamp. So I started thinking about doing bootcamps and classes. After all, people I looked up to and respected where telling me I need to, so I thought I'd better.

That was then my goal. My original goal of training professionals one on one was hijacked by this new goal.

Luckily, I figured out what was going on and stuck to my original goal. Thankfully I did because it has led me to where I am today.

A similar example in business would be that you decide that you're going to focus on direct mail for your marketing. Then your team, your advisors, and people trying to sell you the quick fix solutions start telling you that direct mail is dead. You need to do social media, you need to Tweet this, Facebook that. You need Google AdWords or Facebook ads.

You give in and ditch direct mail and go for what they're telling you to. Your goal gets hijacked.

Now, whether or not these other mediums of marketing work as well or better than direct mail doesn't matter. What matters is that your goal was to use direct mail but outside influences led you to abandon that goal. By the way if you're not currently using direct mail effectively in your business, chances are you're leaving a lot of money on the table. How to use it effectively is one of my core offerings in the Expect Success Academy.

I guess in school our goals are hijacked. When we're kids we dream of being astronauts or musicians or football players but then these dreams are hijacked by our parents, teachers, or peers telling us to 'get real' and that we need to do this or do that instead.

Are you starting to see how goal hijacking can affect you? Think back, have you encountered elements of goal hijacking before? Have your goals been hijacked?

Self-Image

Another roadblock that holds you back is your self-image. The self-image, according to Wikipedia, is defined as:

> *A simple definition of a person's self-image is their answer to the question, "What do you believe people think about you?"*

Self-image may consist of three types:

Self-image resulting from how the individual sees himself or herself.

Self-image resulting from how others see the individual.

Self-image resulting from how the individual perceives others see him or her.

One of the best books available on self-image psychology and one of my favourite books of all time is *Psycho-Cybernetics* by Dr. Maxwell Maltz. Dr. Maltz was a plastic surgeon and discovered the power of self-image psychology after what he thought were successful operations on his patients. In one instance in the book, he describes that he successfully operated on a car crash victim and returned her face to what she looked like before the crash. He exclaimed that this was his best work.

While the woman he had operated on had physically changed for the better, mentally she still felt awful. He discovered that, although he fixed her physical scarring, it was her deep, internal, mental scarring that had the most impact on her happiness.

She had suffered trauma much worse than a car crash, trauma that damaged her self-image. Because of this, no amount of surgery could heal her.

If you haven't read *Psycho-Cybernetics*, I highly recommend you do. It's possibly one of the greatest books ever written on the topic of self-image and personal development.

I, too, suffered some serious self-image scarring when I was growing up. Like I mentioned, I was bullied as a kid and my confidence took a massive knock because of this. There were other life events that left scarring for me. Losing a best friend to suicide was another one.

These events left internal scarring that always made me question what I was doing and the direction I was going. I was always second-guessing my actions, thinking about things way too much, and taking little action.

From reading and studying Dr. Maltz's work as well as applying his techniques, I have overcome my issues and now have a positive self-image, one that helps me rather than hinders me.

You can change on the outside all you want, but until you start to heal the internal scarring you may have, you will always revert back to the way you are. This is because your self-image controls everything. If your self-image is damaged or feels like a failure, then no matter how many times you try to change, you won't be able. Your threats will always get the better of you. You won't change, your business won't change, and your life won't change.

Negative Influences

The last roadblock (and one that can incorporate all of the other roadblocks) is the negative influences you allow into your life. These influences come in many forms and, if you have more negative influences than positive ones, then no matter what you try, you'll ultimately fail. Sometimes our negative influences come from areas of life that may appear harmless.

What are negative influences and how do we deal with them? This is best illustrated by the following example:

EXPECT SUCCESS CYCLE

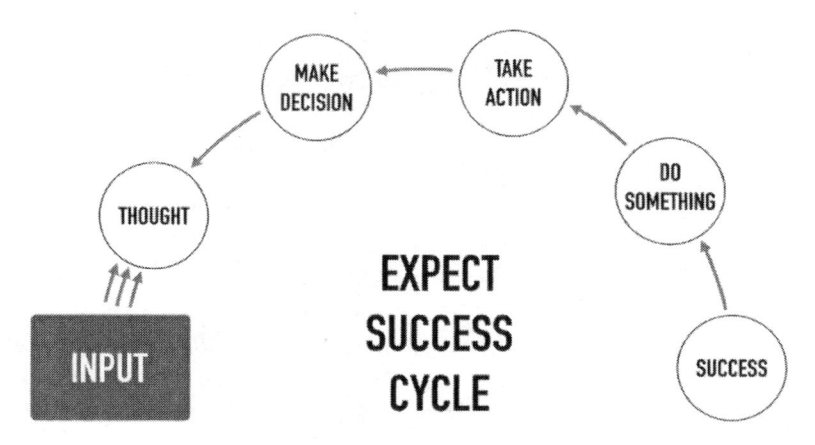

INPUT → THOUGHT → MAKE DECISION → TAKE ACTION → DO SOMETHING → SUCCESS

This is the Expect Success Cycle. I learned a variation of this from Bedros Keuilian, and if I remember correctly, he learned from the excellent and somewhat revered marketer, Frank Kern.

In order to change, you've got to do something, simple as that. To do something, you have to take action. To take action, you've got to make the decision to take action. And of course, any time we make decisions, these decisions are manifested from our thoughts. So here's the Expect Success Cycle in its simplest form: your thoughts lead to your decisions, your decisions lead to your actions, the right actions lead you to doing something worthwhile, something worthwhile leads to success. It's a simple cycle that works.

There's one fundamental problem. Our thoughts are managed by our input. When the wrong input influences your thoughts, the decision, action, do something cycle is completely ruined – absolutely ruined.

Generally speaking, we get our input from news (online or offline), gossip, politics, friends, family, peers, staff, co-workers, partners, competitors, etc. Now, when it comes to news, gossip, and politics, that's nearly always negative input.

The messages we get from them are usually that the world is ruined, you can't trust anyone, and people are inherently bad.

Our other sources of input like friends, family, partners, staff, etc. can also provide negative input (some more than others), which drives home even more negative messages.

Now, with that being the input, how do you think that's going to influence your thoughts? If all the input you're getting is danger, people are bad, etc., what decisions will you make in life? Think about it. Every minute you're making a decision. Will I read this book or not? Will I change? Will I exercise? Will I go to work?

Millions of decisions are being made by your subconscious and conscious mind every day. Remember, your subconscious is the majority part of your mind and thinking capability. So when you've got the news (with all that danger input) on in the background and you think you're not listening, it's entering your subconscious mind and your subconscious controls your thoughts and your decision-making, which leads to your actions, which leads you to making a half-hearted attempt at doing something.

What happens is your thought process will lead you to make the wrong decisions, you'll take the wrong action and make a half-hearted attempt at something, you divert to not doing the right thing, which leads to no success, or failure.

Why? *To support the beliefs that are being instilled by all of your negative influences.*

Are you starting to see how all these roadblocks are connected to your ability to change?

The actions we take have to be congruent with the input we get to support our beliefs. When your input is correctly aligned with your core values, your Expect Success Cycle is complete. You don't pay attention to the noise, nonsense, and negative input variables, and you only listen to what's going to bring you forward – that's when you start to realise that the sky's the limit.

This will become a lot clearer when we start going through the process of overcoming your threat and discovering your core values. You'll start to see more clearly how and why we need to keep tabs on these roadblocks.

Does this make sense?

– 16 –

Define, Refine, and Align

"Let the refining and improving of your own life keep you so busy that you have little time to criticize others."

–H. Jackson Brown, Jr.

Now that we have discussed some of the roadblocks that hold you back, we can talk about the system that I've learned that can enable you to change. Not in a short-term capacity, but in a capacity that is a long-term solution.

The system for long-term and consistent results starts with three short words. Define, Refine, and Align. Before we get into the advanced look at this strategy, let's look at the simplified model.

DEFINE
↓
REFINE
↓
ALIGN

Your Elephant's Under Threat

It never fails. It simply can't. It's based on the idea of identifying and overcoming your 'threat.'

Remember if you're currently unhappy with your business, the way you look, feel, or the direction you're heading, I'm going to hypothesise that you're a losing and you're feeling confused, unfocused, distracted, directionless, uninspired, tired, stressed, alone, slow, un-motivated, isolated, sad, angry, bored, and lost. Essentially, you're feeling threatened.

Here's a more in-depth look at the Define, Refine, and Align model.

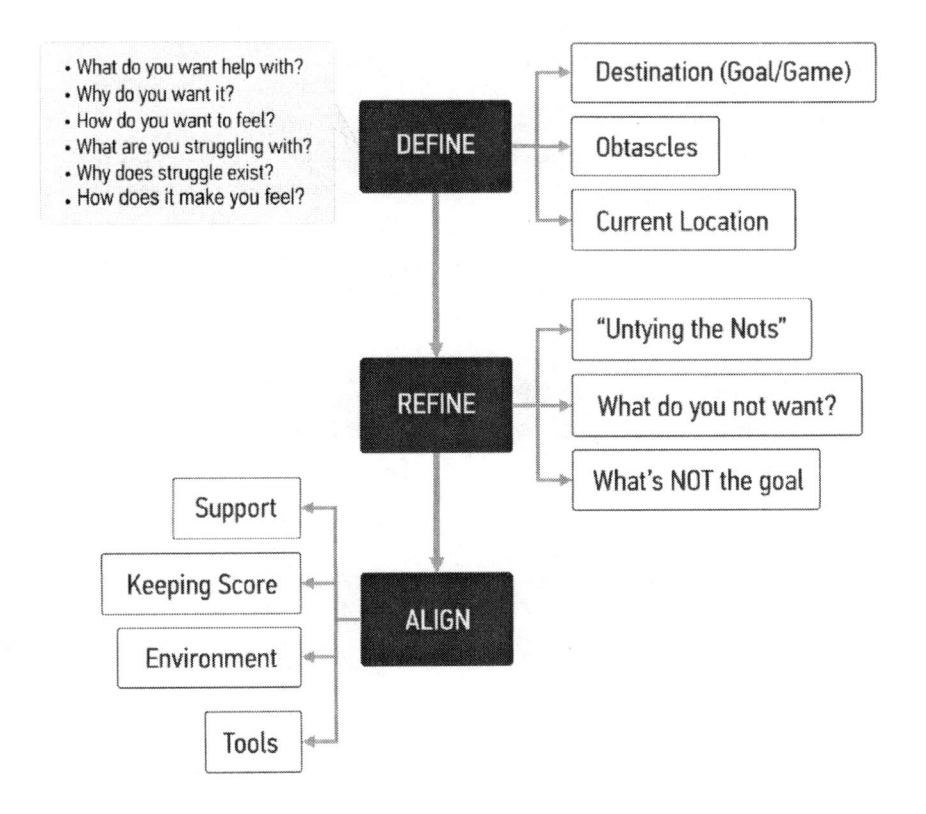

- What do you want help with?
- Why do you want it?
- How do you want to feel?
- What are you struggling with?
- Why does struggle exist?
- How does it make you feel?

DEFINE
- Destination (Goal/Game)
- Obtascles
- Current Location

REFINE
- "Untying the Nots"
- What do you not want?
- What's NOT the goal

ALIGN
- Support
- Keeping Score
- Environment
- Tools

Define, Refine, and Align System

When you follow the system, all of the roadblocks, negative influences, and shiny objects become irrelevant and largely invisible.

If you come across a product, solution, or service that fits with you and will develop your core values and help you achieve your goals (not hijack them), then you invest in them. If they pull you away from your endgame or core values, then they get ignored.

When you understand this process and put it to use, you'll succeed every single time. It's impossible not to.

Why? Because you're playing by *your* rules and *your* parameters in a way that fits *you*. No one else.

You'll have everything stacked in your favour. That's when the magic happens. You know this. When you follow something that *you* control, *you* decided upon, *you* are comfortable with, feed and nurture what works (on an ongoing basis), and refine and test what doesn't, you'll start seeing continuous results quickly *and* over the long-term.

The whole concept of the define, refine, and align system is to help you overcome the number one reason holding you back and preventing you from changing your threats.

– 17 –

It's Not All Mindset, It's Brainset Too

"You become what you believe."

–Oprah Winfrey

To fully understand threat and how it affects your ability to achieve what it is you want to achieve, it's important to understand what 'threat' actually is. This is where brainset philosophy stands to be more important than merely mindset and positive thinking.

Threat starts with the fact that our brains are always seeking homeostasis. Homeostasis is defined as, "a process in which the body's internal environment is kept stable." (Wikipedia)

Our brains and our bodies are always seeking homeostasis. All change threatens homeostasis. All change is therefore threat. Threat can create evolution or devolution, depending upon the levels of strength of the organism.

Threat creates predictable reactions and responses that can be learned and used as tools. In other words, your ability to deal with your threat affects whether or not you'll succeed.

Just so you can fully understand this concept of threat, we need to examine our brain a little bit more in-depth.

We'll start with the Triune Brain Theory, first introduced by Dr. Paul D. Maclean. The Triune Brain Theory is a model of evolution of the vertebrate forebrain. It consists of three areas: the neomammalian complex (neocortex), the paleomammalian complex (limbic system), and the reptilian complex. The theory goes that these structures of the brain were added at different periods of our evolution.

Midbrain
Feel – Remember
Interact with others

Neocortex
Talk – Think – Move
Create - Learn

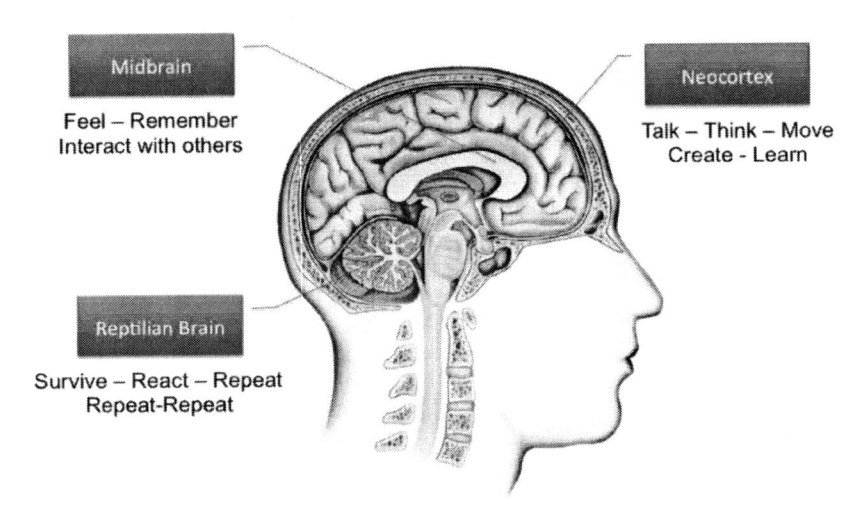

Reptilian Brain
Survive – React – Repeat
Repeat-Repeat

The reptilian complex is responsible for our survival instincts, or the five F's: flight, fight, freeze, feed, and frolic. Three of these F's – fight, flight, and freeze – are the ones we'll be paying close attention to when we start to break down the process of overcoming threat. Our reptilian complex controls basic life functions and actions that take place without thinking. Anything that is a 'threat' causes us to downshift, and when this happens, learning or advancement cannot take place.

The limbic system is responsible for our feelings, motivation, and emotions – it is the goal-driven part of our brain. This part of the brain has visual memory, but language is limited to yells and screams.

The neocortex part of the brain is 76% of the human brain. It is responsible for such things as language, abstraction, reasoning, logic, and meaning. It is the home of academic learning and cognitive thinking.

Now, you may be thinking, *what does all of that have to do with your ability to change or achieve goals?* It has a lot to do with it. When you're under threat, your brain down-shifts and you cannot advance. You cannot achieve.

Remember, our brains constantly crave homeostasis, or in simpler terms, they constantly crave safety. And in order for our brains to feel safe, they need to do two things.

First, they need to assess the situation and predict what's going to happen next.

Secondly, based on these predictions, they develop responses to make sure they reach safety.

When you're under threat, your brain doesn't feel safe, which means there's less certainty, which in turn means that your brain's prediction and ability to respond decreases.

Essentially:

Threat is the inability to predict and respond.

Prediction + response = safety.

No prediction + no response = threat.

Threat is increased through each of our senses and, when registered, they go through the same process of triggering the threat response through the sympathetic nervous system.

Your central nervous system (CNS), reptilian brain, and limbic system work together to create threat response regardless of what the actual threat is. Being under threat is the #1 reason holding you back from changing positively, gaining success, achieving that body, the confidence, and the energy you want and need... so, in order to start moving forward, we need to figure out the threat.

If you want more of what you desire, you need to take care of your threats.

Threat is responded to in three ways. These responses are three of the five F's from the reptilian cortex we discussed a moment ago. They are Fight, Flight, and Freeze.

This concept of fight, flight, and freeze is not a new phenomenon. The fight or flight response was first introduced by Walter Bradford Cannon and is sometimes called, "acute stress response." Here are some examples of the fight, flight, or freeze responses from a traditional perspective.

Fight: imagine a cat walking down a street. Out of nowhere, a dog comes running around and corners the cat. It can't escape. The fight response in the cat would produce an upsurge of adrenaline, causing the cat's awareness to increase, the hairs to stand tall, and the claws to come out.

Similarly, for the flight response in the wild, imagine a gazelle drinking from a watering hole. A lioness comes running out from the nearby trees and immediately the gazelle goes into flight mode. It tears off without even thinking.

The freeze response can similarly be described with the same example. The lioness runs after the gazelle and catches it. The lioness sinks its teeth into the gazelle and throws it about, seemingly killing it. Momentarily, the lioness walks away and the gazelle jumps up, as if waking from a deep freeze, and runs away.

For the purpose of this book and for the purpose of helping you change positively, we will be focusing on the negative effects that these threat responses have on you.

Even though our threat response is an adaptive reaction, the problem for your ability to change comes from *prolonged* exposure to these stresses or threats.

There are a host of physiological, behavioural, and psychological effects that being under threat have on us including headaches, pain, fatigue, no sex drive, lack of sleep, too much sleep, overeating, under-eating, substance abuse, social withdrawal, anxiety, lack of motivation, lack of focus, irritability, anger, restlessness, and depression.

That list isn't all-inclusive, but hopefully it starts to paint a very clear picture of why you're not able to achieve what it is you want to achieve.

The whole idea of mindset becomes largely irrelevant in comparison to the effect that being threatened can have on your ability to achieve your goals. You can try and think as positively as you can, but if you're under threat and your body downshifts, it's going to be of no use – you simply won't be able to change; your brain won't allow it.

It can't because it doesn't feel safe.

When you're looking to change or to achieve goals, you first need to discover where the threat is, then overcome it. The process of doing so isn't very complicated. I wanted to explain the whole idea of threat just so you would have a foundation which we could work from.

Again, our threats are responded to in three ways: fight, flight, or freeze.

The fight response is one of anger, aggression, and obvious resistance. The language you use is all negative and aggressive. Words like, "Can't," "No," and, "Won't," are used and you refuse to take advice.

The flight response is one of evasiveness. It is one of rapid withdrawal and immediately dismissing your goals and discontinuing the pursuit of them. Oftentimes, the flight response can be staged withdrawal through excuses for not doing things, procrastination, absenteeism, lateness, or presenteeism.

The freeze response is one of complete inaction. You have that feeling of being stuck, you feel you can't change, or you're too fearful too change.

The idea of the threat response becomes even more powerful when we explain it in combination with one of Tony Robbins' core pillars of Personal Power. Personal Power had a groundbreaking impact (and still does) on my development and is something I've learned an awful lot from.

In *Personal Power II*, Tony talks about the desire to gain pleasure and avoid pain. That sums up everyone in a nutshell. Everyone, no matter who you are, has two desires:

- Gain pleasure
- Avoid pain

Everything we do in life is because we're looking to either gain pleasure or avoid pain.

Our threat responses (whether it's fight, flight, or freeze) are directly related to these two needs. Remember, if we go into fight, flight, or freeze mode, it is because our brains are seeking homeostasis or safety.

When you cannot change or you're struggling to get started with something, it is because you associate more pain to changing than pleasure. Why do you associate more pain to it than pleasure? Because you're under threat.

Threat is predominantly belief-based, so if you believe X but read or listen to something in opposition to X, by default it's an attack on your beliefs, but by extension, an attack on you.

Here's an example.

Say you were brought up to believe that breakfast is the most important meal of the day. You were brought up to believe that you need to eat first thing in the morning. You've eaten breakfast every morning for as long as you can remember. After all, it's what everyone else does and it's what you've been taught to do.

Then one day, after looking in the mirror, you realise that you've let yourself go slightly and you need to drop a few pounds. Being the resourceful type, you head over to the Google machine and you start looking for solutions.

There's a lot of information and you come across something called intermittent fasting. The type of fasting you start reading about promotes pre-defined meal skipping and not eating your first meal until at least 12:00 pm. Now, whether or not intermittent fasting works doesn't matter, it's what the idea of fasting might do to your belief that does.

Since you were brought up to believe that breakfast is the most important meal of the day and you must eat first thing in the morning, the idea of fasting and skipping breakfast threatens your beliefs... until you overcome that threat, it won't be an effective eating style for you. By default, this won't sit well with you because it's an attack on your beliefs and an attack on you. You've lost even before the game has started.

Threat is caused by three things: something is either too fast, too slow, or has unclear intent.

Too fast: If you're trying to change too quickly, it can cause greater uncertainty and overstimulation. This causes your bucket to fill rapidly and overflow.

Too slow: You fear that your desired outcome won't be forthcoming and any investment, whether it's time or money, will be wasted.

Unclear intent: When you're unsure of what kind of outcome it will have on your life or you're unsure of the why behind it, then this becomes a threat.

As a small experiment, take a few minutes to examine what areas of your life currently feel too fast, too slow, or unclear. Get out a piece of paper and a pen and write down your thoughts about this for greater clarity.

Thankfully, threat can be dissipated by investigation. When you start to eliminate the threat in your life, then you can start changing, start associating more pleasure than pain, and start achieving your goals.

And that's exactly what I'm going to show you now.

- 18 -

Basic Define, Refine, and Align Pathway

"Too many of us are not living our dreams because we are living our fears."

–Les Brown

Every successful change (life, physical, or otherwise) comes from identifying and overcoming your threats. There are essentially three core elements we are working on when we go through this process. These three elements ensure that you will be successful.

Core Pathways:

- The ability to define *exactly* what it is you want. (Define)
- The ability to refine that goal and find out what it's *not*. (Refine)
- The ability to *correctly* align yourself to that goal. (Align)

This is essentially the Define, Refine and Align model we discussed. Now we're going to break that down and go through each part in detail.

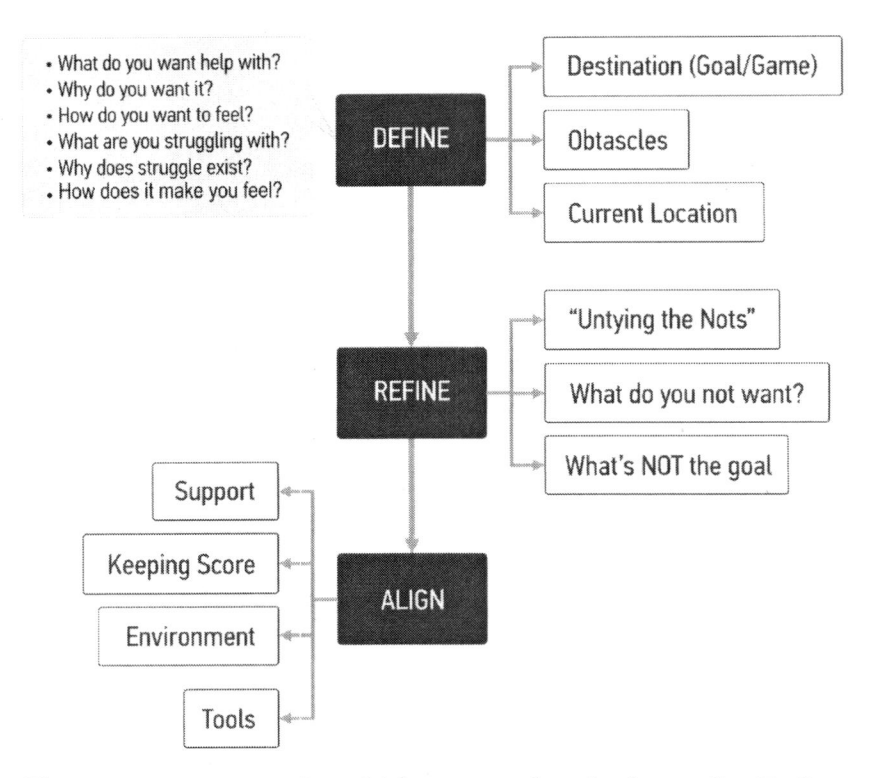

- What do you want help with?
- Why do you want it?
- How do you want to feel?
- What are you struggling with?
- Why does struggle exist?
- How does it make you feel?

DEFINE
→ Destination (Goal/Game)
→ Obtascles
→ Current Location

REFINE
→ "Untying the Nots"
→ What do you not want?
→ What's NOT the goal

ALIGN
← Support
← Keeping Score
← Environment
← Tools

There are two ways in which we can break down the Define, Refine, and Align model – the basic framework (which is above) and the advanced framework. We're going to be discussing both ways, but we'll start with the basic framework.

Define, Refine, and Align Basic Model for Change

Define

We need to define exactly what it is that you want. This is the end goal or endgame. We also need to define what the obstacles preventing you from achieving it are. Finally, we need to be clear as to where you are currently in respect to your desired goal.

Some questions that you can ask yourself to start defining these three things are:

- What do you want help with?
- Why do you want it?
- How do you want to feel?
- What are you currently struggling with?
- Why do you think this struggle exists?
- How does it make you feel?
- What obstacles are preventing you from achieving it?
- What have you tried? What has worked and what hasn't?
- Where are you now in relation to your goal?
- What progress have you made?
- On a scale of 1-10, where are you in regards to achieving it?

Refine

The refine process is where we dig in a little deeper and go through the process of 'untying the nots.' This is where we go through the process of defining exactly what it is we do *not* want. Here we're looking to figure out what's *not* the goal. A good exercise for you to do is to write down everything you don't want.

From looking at everything that you don't want, we will then have a better picture of everything that you *do* want.

For illustration purposes, I'll provide two examples.

Example A is a business owner who wants to change. We'll call him Bob. Bob has been working 60-80 hours a week in his business for the last 22 years and he's looking to change. He just doesn't get any joy out of his business anymore. He feels trapped and he's sick and tired of not being able to spend time with his family and do the things he enjoys.

Bob's 'untying the nots' exercise might look like something like this:

- Doesn't want to work 80 hours every week.
- Doesn't want to have to get up early every morning and drive an hour to the office.
- Doesn't want to have to do everything himself.
- Doesn't want to have to sacrifice his family life for his business.
- Doesn't want to work weekends.
- Doesn't want to make phone calls.
- Doesn't want to feel like his business is a job more than an actual business.
- Doesn't want to have to worry about whether or not he'll have enough money to retire.
- Doesn't want to be a failure.
- Doesn't want to let his family down.
- Doesn't want to have to close his business.
- Doesn't want to give less than 100% to his customers.

From looking at Bob's list of things he doesn't want, it starts to paint a pretty clear picture of what he *does* want.

Example B is a depressed, overweight woman called Jane. Jane's untying the nots exercise might look something like this:

- Doesn't want to feel trapped by her weight.
- Doesn't want to go to a gym because she feels she won't fit in.
- Doesn't want to diet because she's tried them all and they didn't work.
- Doesn't want surgery because she thinks it's a cop out.
- Doesn't want to end up with diabetes or worse.
- Doesn't want to end up alone.
- Doesn't want to feel embarrassed every time she eats in public.
- Doesn't want to be stared at when she tries to exercise.
- Doesn't want to be labelled by her weight.

- Doesn't want to have to spend excess money on expensive clothes that make her look fat.
- Doesn't want to die.

Again, looking at Jane's list of things that she doesn't want really hones in on the fact that it's about more than just losing weight.

Align

Once we define what it is we do want and then combine it with what it is we don't want, the final stage is to align ourselves with what or who can take us there.

Two initial questions to ask yourself in the alignment phase are:

- What do you need to start doing?
- What do you need to stop doing?

Some more questions you may think about asking are:

- What are your options?
- What could you do differently?
- Do you know someone who has encountered a similar situation?
- What small step can you take today?

(Some questions taken from *Coaching for Performance*, 4th Edition: GROWing Human Potential and Purpose and People Skills for Professionals.)

This process of alignment is the most important for me personally. It sets the stage, and answering the right questions as well as aligning with the right tools, resources, and people will help make your goals much easier to achieve. This will become even more apparent when we discuss the system in-depth, which we will do now.

John Mulry, MSc

– 19 –

Advanced Define, Refine, and Align Pathways

"The person who says it cannot be done should not interrupt the person who is doing it."

–Chinese Proverb

The basic model of the define, refine, and align process will work in most instances, but to fully grasp just how powerful it can be, we will examine it from a big picture perspective.

The stages of overcoming threat then become:

1. Define the goal or endgame
2. Create, understand, and play by your rules
3. Create the environment
4. Keep score
5. Find support

This is where the beauty of this system becomes unique to you *every time*. If we use the analogy of the bucket again, we can see how this process works effectively in helping us change. We start with identifying our threat, then working to overcome it. If you look at the following image, it will paint a picture of what the actual process looks like.

We can also look at this in the context of 'emptying our bucket.'

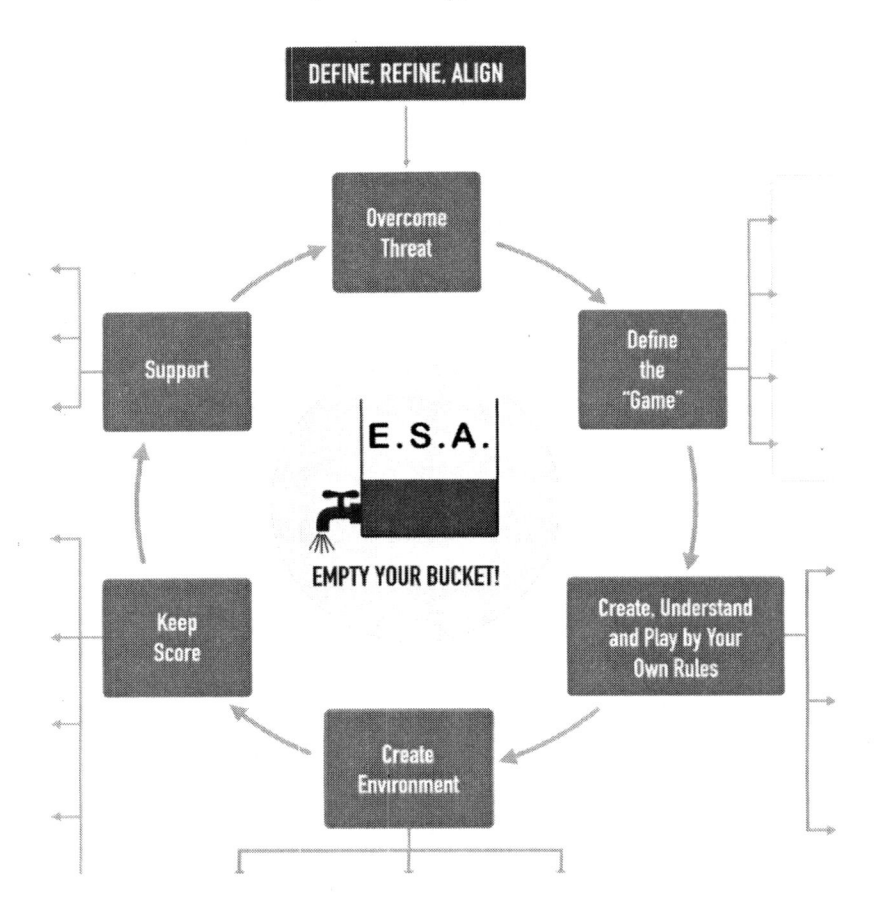

Here's what the advanced version looks like with everything tacked on:

Your Elephant's Under Threat

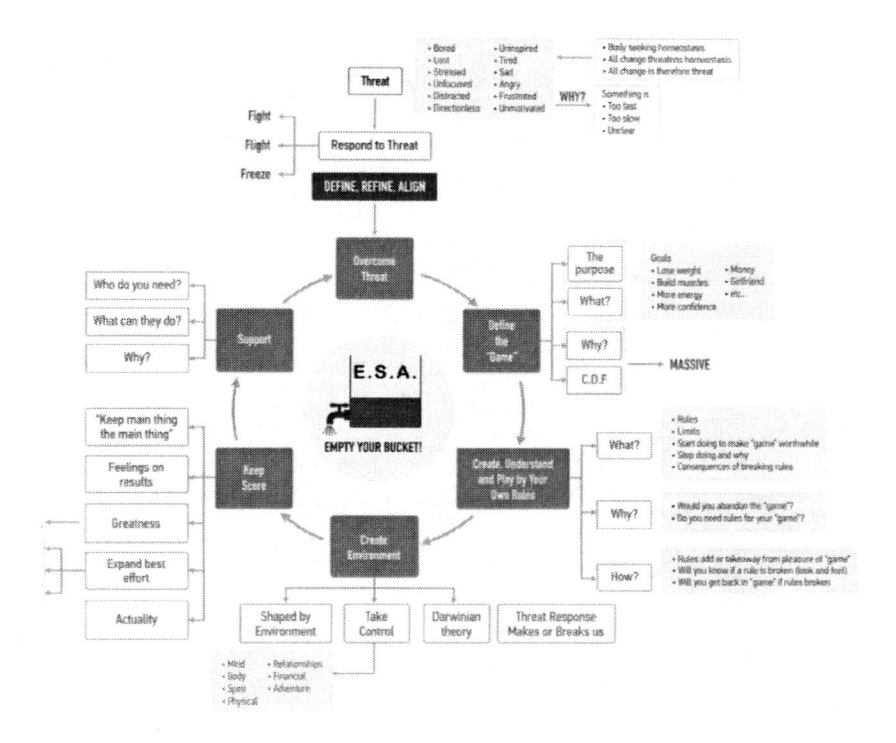

Obviously, looking at the advanced system as a whole can be daunting, which is why we examine each component as its own self-contained system.

We will now go in-depth to each part of the system and go through each stage step by step. By doing so I will be providing you with a roadmap you can follow, one you can use whenever you come up against difficulty.

1. **Identify the Threat**

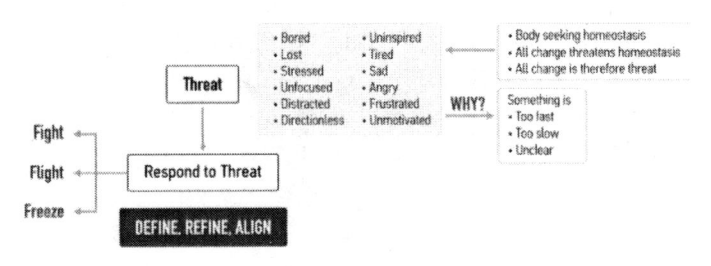

It's important to remember that the end goal is to overcome the threat holding us back. The threat response is always going to be fight, flight, or freeze, so we first need to identify what is too fast, too slow, or unclear. The size of the threat doesn't matter; it's the effect it has on our ability to act that matters. By first identifying the threat, we can then work to overcome it.

2. Define the Goal or Endgame:

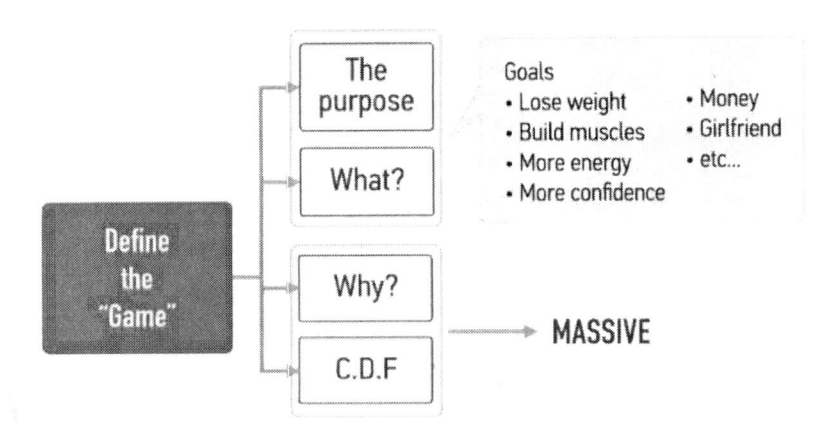

```
                    ┌──────────┐    Goals
                 ┌─▶│   The    │    • Lose weight    • Money
                 │  │ purpose  │    • Build muscles  • Girlfriend
                 │  └──────────┘    • More energy    • etc...
                 │  ┌──────────┐    • More confidence
                 ├─▶│  What?   │
 ┌─────────┐     │  └──────────┘
 │ Define  │     │
 │   the   │─────┤  ┌──────────┐
 │ "Game"  │     ├─▶│   Why?   │─────▶ MASSIVE
 └─────────┘     │  └──────────┘
                 │  ┌──────────┐
                 └─▶│   C.D.F  │
                    └──────────┘
```

What?

In order for you to positively change or to achieve anything, you must first get clear about what it is you want. The more specific you can be here, the better. You have to really hone in on what the purpose of what you want to achieve is. This is more than just wanting to lose weight or earn more money. Really hone in on the specifics.

It took me a long time to realise this. Remember, I had no direction, I had no real reason for doing the things I did, and any reason I thought of was superficial, lame, and not worthwhile. Looking back it's like trying to use sat-nav or GPS to get somewhere but not actually telling the sat-nav where you want to go. It just didn't make sense.

Tom Hopkins defines success as, "*the continuous pursuit towards pre-determined worthwhile goals.*" The two keywords there are "pre-determined" and "worthwhile." Before you set out to change positively and overcome your threat, define clearly what it is you want to achieve. You can use the S.M.A.R.T. (Specific, Measurable, Attainable, Relevant, and Time-Based) acronym for goal-setting if you want, but honestly you don't have to be that anal about it. Just pick a goal and make sure it's worthwhile.

Some questions you can ask yourself are:

- What do you want to achieve?
- What areas do you need help with?
- Describe in detail exactly what you want.
- What is the purpose here? What are you really here for?

I must stress that being generic here won't help – the more specific you can be, the better. Take Bob, for example (our example from before). If he said his goal was that he wanted more free time – that's pretty generic.

If Bob were to say, "I want to work 30 hours a week, have at least two days off a week, and be able to spend eight weeks out of the year on holidays with my family. I want to be able to golf on weekends."

Bob is being pretty specific about what he wants. We know that he wants:

- A 30-hour work week
- To work five days per week
- Eight weeks of holidays per year
- Time for golfing on the weekends

That's much better than just saying, "I want more time."

Why?

The next stage of the goal comes from defining why you want it. You need to be clear about why you want what you want. This is arguably the most important part of the process. It gives your goal meaning. Something you can hold on to and look to when the times get tough. If your goal is worthwhile, chances are the going will be tough on your journey to achieving it, so having a powerful reason why is imperative. Think of it as the internal fire keeping you going no matter what.

Taking the second example we used of Jane who wants to lose weight, imagine that you are Jane and your goal is to lose weight.

Your reason why is going to be way more than just wanting to lose weight. Your reason why might be:

- You want to be healthy enough to walk your daughter down the aisle on her wedding day.
- You want to be fit and healthy enough to play sports with your kids and enjoy life.
- You want to feel a new vigour and lease of life to build self-confidence to do the things you've never done.
- It could be that you're sick and tired of feeling trapped by your body.
- You're fed up because you can't go on holidays because you're too big for an airplane.
- You're tired of being embarrassed every time you eat something.
- You don't want to end up alone.

Whatever your why is – once you know what it is – that's when you can start working towards it. And most importantly, at a pace that suits you and you alone. Sure, you might need a push every now and again. But don't compare your progress to anyone else's but your own. You only ever have to compete with yourself from yesterday. Self-improvement is the name of the game.

So how do you determine your reason why? Questions you might ask are:

- What are you looking to achieve?
- Why do you want to achieve it?
- What is it about the goal that is important to you?
- If you achieve said goal, how will your life change? What will be different? How will it impact you?
- What is it about not achieving this goal that frightens you?

I'll start off with a generic example stating, "I want to lose weight."

Q. What are you looking to achieve?

A. I want to lose weight.

Q. Why do you want to lose weight?

A. Well, I know that I'm heavier than I should be and would like to change.

Q. What is it about changing that is important to you?

A. I'm getting to the age my father was when he died and I'd like to live a lot longer.

Q. If you lose the weight, how will your life change? What will be different? How will it impact you?

A. It'll mean that I'll get healthier but also that I'll be able to watch my kids grow up and not worry if I'll be around to see them flourish.

Q. What is it about not losing weight that frightens you?

A. The thought of not seeing my kids grow up is frightening and I don't want to end up the way my dad did.

You see now that it's much more than just wanting to lose weight. There's an internal reason why. The fire is lit, and with the right guidance, you can become unstoppable in your quest. There will be ups and downs along the way; success is by no means linear. But when you determine your "why"- your true reason why - you're ensuring that you're taking the path of least resistance toward success.

Once we've determined the reason why, we've started the process of translating the goal into a feeling. A goal is exactly that – a goal. But a feeling is something powerful, something real within us.

Core Desired Feeling

Outspoken author Danielle LaPorte defines goals as checkpoints to core desired feelings, and I agree with her. When we strive to achieve goals, it's not the goal itself we crave, it's the feeling we get on the journey to achieving it and when we achieve it. So, by tapping into the core desired feeling behind our goals and looking to align with that feeling consistently, the process of achieving it becomes infinitely easier.

Think of it in terms of cause and effect. The cause is the feeling, the effect is the goal.

Ask yourself questions like these to really hone in on your core desired feelings:

- How will you feel once you achieve your goal?
- Why do you want to feel this way?
- Have you felt that way before?
- What does it mean to you to feel this way?
- When you say you feel _____, what do you mean?

Tapping into your reason why and your core desired feeling are massive. These steps are often missed by many, but they are crucial. You may be thinking this is a lot of work to go through, and in some respects it is, but aren't you worth it?

Brian Grasso, author of *Audacity of Success* and founder of the Free Thinking Renegades Nation, described this process to me perfectly when I interviewed him in my research for this book.

In the interview, we were talking about the fact that people tend to focus more on the *how* or *what* behind their goals than the actual *why* behind them. Sure, you do need to know what it is you want, but if you don't uncover the true reason *why* you want something, you'll be more susceptible to goal hijacking and doing things for the wrong reasons like I did. Up until a few years ago, I was constantly chasing after goals I thought were my own. In reality, they weren't. It wasn't until I started tapping into my own reasons why and started translating my goals into the core desired feelings behind them that everything became clear.

My own reason why for doing things is quite simple and I wish to share that with you today:

I want to instill the expect success attitude in you and show you that you can achieve everything you want in business and in life. I want this because, by helping others achieve, I will achieve great success myself, and doing so will give me the freedom, control, and time to spend with those who matter most in my life – my girlfriend Jess, my mother, my sister, my friends, and my dog Oscar.

Now, everything I do is aimed towards my reason why. When the roadblocks come up (and there are plenty), I simply refer back to my reason why and my core desired feelings behind it and I get the strength to smash through those roadblocks.

3. Create, Understand, and Play by Your Rules

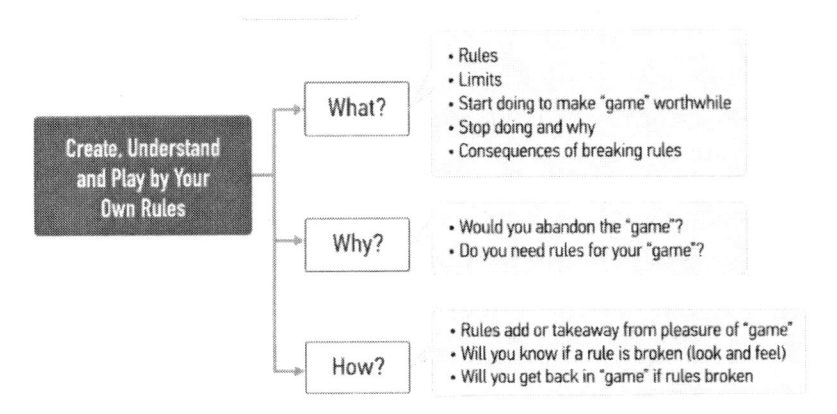

Create, Understand and Play by Your Own Rules

- **What?**
  - Rules
  - Limits
  - Start doing to make "game" worthwhile
  - Stop doing and why
  - Consequences of breaking rules

- **Why?**
  - Would you abandon the "game"?
  - Do you need rules for your "game"?

- **How?**
  - Rules add or takeaway from pleasure of "game"
  - Will you know if a rule is broken (look and feel)
  - Will you get back in "game" if rules broken

The next stage of the process is where some of the real fun starts. Fun? Really? Yep, who says change or goal achievement should be boring? It doesn't need to be. This stage is where we define the rules of our goals or game. We get to set the rules and thus we get control over our ability to change.

This step is important because when you are in control of your destiny, it offers a freedom that's really rewarding.

Another reason why this step is important is because we gain ownership of the goals, we start to build an internal accountability system that ties the success of changing to the most important person there is – you. Sure, as you see in later stages we will be looking to different support structures, but when you follow something that *you* control, *you* decided upon, *you* are comfortable with, it makes everything internal and right for *you*.

Three areas we focus on when setting the rules of our game are:

- What
- Why

Your Elephant's Under Threat

- How

Don't confuse the what and the why here with those in step two. We have already determined what it is we want to achieve and why we want to achieve it. The what and the why here are based around the rules that make achieving it worthwhile. See, like I said, fun.

Why do we need rules?

Defining rules for our goals acts as a safety net or comfort blanket. You'll know when things are going off course or when you're starting to go astray. Rules also help in minimising any attempts for outside forces to hijack our goals. Another big reason for developing rules is that they help us fill our self-esteem bank account, which comes into play in step 5.

Why:

- Why do you need rules?
- Why would you abandon your goal?

What:

- What rules can you put in place to make sure you stay committed?
- What do you need to stop doing and why?
- What are the consequences of not stopping this?
- What do you need to start doing to make the goal worthwhile?
- What are the consequences of not starting this?
- What will happen if you break these rules?

How:

- How do your rules add or take away from your goal?
- How will you know if a rule is broken?
- How will you get back on track if a rule is broken?

Essentially what you will be doing here is defining some initial action points as well as setting up the criteria that help keep you on track.

The three most critical questions are:

- What do you need to stop doing and why?
- What do you need to start doing to make the goal worthwhile?
- How will you get back on track if a rule is broken?

The first question sets the stage to make way for your success. What do you need to stop doing and why? Oftentimes we cannot begin something until we make room for it. Our lives are hectic and we have only a certain amount of space and time for things. Otherwise the goal we want to achieve will only fill up our bucket more, causing us to feel overwhelmed and eventually give in.

Dax Moy calls this releasing the brakes and I think it's a perfect analogy. Think of your life as a car. One foot is on the accelerator trying to go full speed ahead. Problem is, your other foot is on the brakes, holding you back from getting to where you need to be. You cannot move forward until you take your foot off the brakes. Makes sense, right?

Or think of it this way. Imagine a child who wants a new toy. In order for the child to get a new toy, he must first give up an old toy to make way for the new one.

Before you can actively start working towards your goal, you must first set some rules and stop doing the things that are like brakes holding you back.

The second question is about winning. What do you need to start doing? This question leads you to defining what action you can start taking towards your goal. The beauty here is that the action can be anything, because you're defining it in relation to achieving your goal. Why is this important? Any positive action is good. Think of it this way:

Action > Excitement > Passion > Purpose

So, should you go hell for leather all at once? No, there's no need. What you're aiming for here is the small win.

One of the biggest stumbling blocks people face when setting out on their journey of change is waiting for everything to be perfect, for the stars to align and *bam!* That's when they'll start. Has this happened to you? You decide you'll do something to change your life, you'll redevelop your marketing strategy, you'll start working out, you'll clean up your diet, or you'll hire a coach – then you think:

"I'll start tomorrow, or I'll start Monday – I'll just get everything organised and then I'll start."

This problem is the biggest around holidays (especially New Year's) but always seems to present itself on weekends – we get an idea to completely change our lives for the better, then that little guy sitting on our shoulder whispers in our ear, "Wait until tomorrow or just finish off the last of the chips, cookies, and chocolate and start Monday."

What tends to happen is that you get so caught up in all these finer details that you start creating more and more obstacles for yourself, right? This is a form of procrastination at best, but at worst it comes down to fear.

We fear starting something new because we don't know how things will turn out so we try to get everything in order so we know we'll get off to the best start possible. Problem is, this is what holds us back rather than pushing us forward.

Let me illustrate.

I used to try and get all my ducks in a row before starting anything. I'd make sure that every minor detail was in place (I believed it was down to my apparent attention to detail – boy was I wrong!) before beginning anything. It was only when I began to look at the things I *said I would start*, and comparing them to what I *actually started* that I noticed the gulf in difference.

Where am I going wrong? I thought. I had the best of intentions but just couldn't seem to get going. After consulting with one of my mentors, I realized the problem – I was striving for perfection when it doesn't exist.

Instead, what I should've focused on and what I'd like you to focus on is taking some action – specifically *imperfect* action – towards your goal. Don't wait for the stars to align, just do something! Action breeds success – thinking about action doesn't.

The analogy I like to use is from the book of the same name by Michael Masterson, *Ready Fire Aim*.

Don't wait for everything to be perfect – take imperfect action and course correct along the way. Back when I was launching my first website, the design was shoddy and was far from perfect, but I launched it anyway so I could start spreading my message and sharing my ideas. Today, I am where I am because of that imperfect action. It's still not perfect, but it's not supposed to be! As long as I constantly strive to improve upon it, that's all that matters.

The question, "What can I start doing?" will enable you to do the same with your goals. You'll be able to define exactly what it is you can do, no matter how big or small. Start doing something today, anything that will take you closer to your goal. Then do another thing the next day – keep course correcting and taking consistent imperfect action and you'll be on the road to success. It really is that simple.

As I mentioned, action breeds success. Not only that, but action breeds action – when you do something, you get a result. You mightn't always get the result you want, but you get something – and as they say, something is better than nothing.

Best of all, by answering the question yourself, it is you who defines what you should be doing, no one else.

The third question, "How will you get back on track if a rule is broken?" helps you when things get difficult.

I'm not going to tell you that everything is going to be rosy and you won't come against any challenges. Like I said, if your goal is worthwhile, chances are there will be more than one or two hiccups along the way.

By asking yourself this question, you are giving yourself permission to slip up in a way that won't derail you completely. You are essentially instilling the trait of perseverance. I used to give up at the first sign of struggle; if I didn't get what I wanted I would give up and think, *Well, I tried, I'm just not good enough.* How did that serve me? Not so well.

What if Thomas Edison gave up on the 9,999th time? What if Victor E. Frankl gave up when he was suffering in Auschwitz? There are many instances in history where giving up was a lot easier than persevering.

I remember the day I nearly quit training altogether. I'd been training and training and the little results I'd seen had dwindled, so I said to myself, "What's the use?" I quit... well, nearly quit. I'm a firm believer in the saying, "things happen for a reason."

At that time I was reading my favourite book, *Think and Grow Rich* by Napoleon Hill, and I can remember exactly what I was reading because it was so relevant to my situation. I was reading the story *Three Feet from Gold*.

Essentially the story goes that a gold miner gave up just three feet from hitting the jackpot. If he had persisted, he would have succeeded. This question allows you to set the rules that you will follow if you come up short. By doing so, you cannot fail. You're defining what it is you will do if you become stuck.

For example, some answers might be:

"How will you get back on track if a rule is broken?"

- I will examine what I was doing right.
- I will examine what I was doing wrong and what I can do to fix it.
- I will seek help in someone who has experienced a similar situation.
- I will refer back to my reason why for inspiration.
- I will immediately do something to get me back on track.

Setting the rules is a critical (and fun) part of the process and one that will enable you to:

- Create the space so you can move forward.
- Decide on some initial action steps.
- Give yourself permission to slip up and decide how you will get back on track.

After you set the rules for your success, the next step is to create the environment that will best serve you and help you align with the tools, resources, and people you need to succeed.

4. Create the Environment

Your Elephant's Under Threat

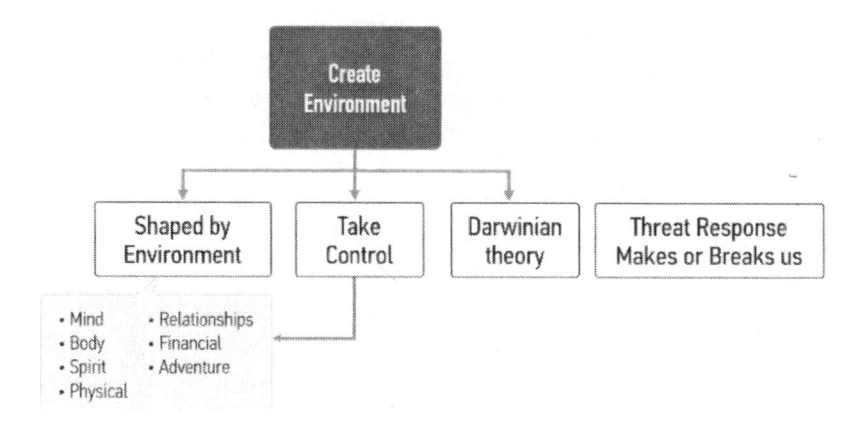

```
                    Create
                 Environment
        ┌───────────┬───────────┬───────────┐
   Shaped by      Take      Darwinian   Threat Response
  Environment    Control     theory    Makes or Breaks us

  • Mind    • Relationships
  • Body    • Financial
  • Spirit  • Adventure
  • Physical
```

Creating our environment helps us align with what we need, but also helps us define what we don't need or want. This is where the process of untying the nots that we discussed earlier works well. Remember, by untying the nots we are effectively deciding on what our environment will look like.

We are shaped by our environment, whether that's where we go, what we surround ourselves with, or whom we surround ourselves with.

A perfect example here is Jane. Jane's goal is weight loss related, so if her environment is fast food restaurants, sweets, biscuits, fried foods, and friends or family members that encourage her to overeat and indulge, how will that affect Jane's ability to lose weight?

She may succeed, but it's gong to be a monumental task. Now if Jane's environment is one of healthy meals, fresh fruit, vegetables, lean meats, and healthy fats as well as regular physical exercise, a support community, coach, and people who have achieved what Jane wants, how will that affect Jane's chances of success?

With this kind of environment, Jane would find it very difficult *not* to succeed.

How we shape our environment determines the function of it. The beauty is that we can shape our environment easily. By doing so, we are taking control. When we are in control of our environment, we are in complete control of the outcome.

Going back to the analogy of the bucket, our environment can be the tap that either fills our bucket or empties our bucket.

If your environment is one that fills your bucket, at best you will find it extremely difficult to succeed and at worst your bucket will collapse and overflow no matter what you try.

On the other hand, if your environment serves to empty your bucket then your ability to change becomes infinitely easier. Think of your environment as the tap. It can be placed above your bucket and fill it up, or it can be on the side of your bucket, emptying it.

Areas of your environment that you may need to address are:

Self – Mind, body, and spirit. These can be thoughts that occupy your mind, how you treat you body, and your bigger picture.

Physical – This is the world around you and the places and things you associate and surround yourself with.

Relationships – These are the people you associate with.

Financial – How are you spending your money?

Adventure – How do you unwind? What do you do for adventure?

The first three above are linked to the type of support structure you have, which we will be discussing in step six.

The best way to create and shape your environment is by aligning with what you want and honing in on what you don't want. By going through the untying the nots exercise, you will know exactly what you don't want. Keeping this front and centre will cause you to create an environment that serves you instead of hindering you.

Questions you may also want to ask yourself are:

- What are the thoughts I need to focus on?
- What kind of attitude do I need to have?
- What can I do to improve how I think about things?
- How can I spend my time more wisely?
- Does my body serve me in the best way possible? If not, what can I do to improve it?
- Who are the people in my life that are currently holding me back?
- What can I do to minimise the impact they have on me?
- Who do I know who has achieved what I want to achieve?
- Where can I find them?
- What kind of places do they visit?
- Are there groups I can join?
- Are there areas of my life where I am throwing away money?

Creating your environment may mean that you have to answer some hard questions. Your environment plays a big role in your success. Once you have your environment, the next step is to know how to keep score.

5. Decide on How You Will Keep Score

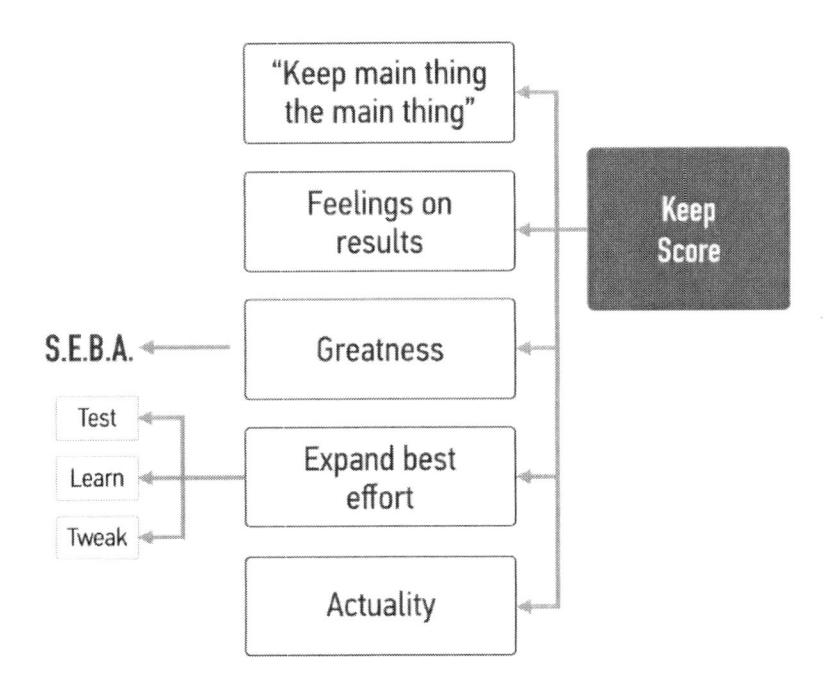

```
                    "Keep main thing
                     the main thing"  ←┐
                                       │
                     Feelings on       │
                      results     ←────┤      ┌──────────┐
                                       │      │   Keep   │
                                       ├──────│  Score   │
  S.E.B.A. ←────     Greatness    ←────┤      │          │
  ┌──────┐                              │      └──────────┘
  │ Test │←┐                            │
  └──────┘ │         Expand best        │
  ┌──────┐ │          effort       ←────┤
  │ Learn│←┤                            │
  └──────┘ │                            │
  ┌──────┐ │                            │
  │ Tweak│←┘         Actuality     ←────┘
  └──────┘
```

This step of the process is really straight forward. Keeping score enables you to know if what you're doing is working or not. It helps you hone in on the things that are going great and find out what's not working so you can either change things slightly or switch them up completely.

Keeping score also plays a huge role in our brainset (not just mindset, remember). Keeping score is like a drug for our brains. The drug we're addicted to here is dopamine. We are all by nature goal-seeking organisms. We will always strive to achieve goals, and when we do, we get a dopamine release in our brains.

Dopamine functions as a neurotransmitter and it plays a big role in our reward and motivation behaviours. Dopamine is triggered by every type of reward we get and, in fact, many illegal drugs are based on increasing the effects of dopamine.

Research was done at MIT by Professor Ann Graybiel on the effects of dopamine. This research was different from previous research on dopamine as it focused on long-term goals instead of short-term goals.

The researchers trained rats to find their way through a maze, and for doing so, they would be rewarded with some chocolate. The idea behind this was one of delayed gratification.

The results of these tests were:

Dopamine levels increased steadily and were at their highest as the rat reached the chocolate, which suggests that the rats anticipated the chocolate, according to the researchers.

Furthermore, they added that, unlike previous studies, the level of dopamine release was not dependent on the speed and duration of the trial or the probability that the rat would get the chocolate.

Professor Ann Graybiel of the McGovern's Institute for Brain research at MIT said:

"Instead, the dopamine signal seems to reflect how far away the rat is from its goal. The closer it gets, the stronger the signal becomes."

Professor Graybiel also mentioned that the size of the reward was linked to the size of the dopamine signal. This supports the notion that your goals should be worthwhile. The bigger and more worthwhile your goals are, the better. She also went on to say:

"This 'internal guidance system' could also be useful for humans, who also have to make choices along the way to what may be a distant goal."

So, by keeping score, we will be able to tune in to our own 'internal guidance system' to help us when our goals seem distant.

Keeping score will help us keep the goal in our mind all the time, thus making it easier for us to stay on track, thus making it easier for us to achieve it.

Imagine a game of football. The two teams are going hell for leather. Both teams' defenses are having nightmares and their offenses are on fire, scoring all around them. Now imagine the same game with no rules, no structure, and no way of keeping score. How would you know who won? You wouldn't. The game would be pointless.

That is why we must have rules, must have structure, and must be able to keep score.

Why you must keep score:

- To know if you're winning. The first point is straight forward and leads on to the rest. By keeping track of your goals, you'll easily know if what you're doing is working or not.
- To keep the main thing the main thing. Keeping score means you won't lose sight. You get to keep your core desired feeling and reason why front and centre and not get distracted by any shiny objects, hijackers, or anything that's going to pull you away from achieving or changing.
- To hone in on what's working best. You can focus the majority of your efforts on what's working the best. Think of the 80/20 rule. 80% of your results will come from 20% of what you do. By focusing on what's working, you get to swing these percentages in your favour.
- To fix or abandon what's not working. Einstein defined insanity as, *"doing the same thing over and over and expecting a different result."* Keeping score enables you to find out exactly what is working and what's not working. Then you can test and tweak the elements that are not working until they start working. You'll also be in a better position to abandon elements that are not

working by applying the time intensity curve formula to them. Is the payoff worth the time you are investing in them? If not, it may be time to try something else. You wouldn't know this if you weren't keeping score.
- To maintain accountability. Internal accountability is important. It keeps you grounded and, again, it serves to help you keep your goal front and centre. The next stage of support brings in external accountability, but you also need internal measures. Keeping score consistently is the easiest form of accountability there is.

If we were to bring everything together with an example, it would look something like this:

Let's say I had a goal of increasing my sales online by 20% in the next month. The action I take is to run an online marketing campaign that has multiple different sources of leads. If I were to just put up a lot of different sources with no way of measuring what was working and what wasn't, I may get some results but I would have no way of determining where the results were coming from.

Now say I still have the exact same goal, but this time I define the rules along with it and create the environment.

Keeping score here might look like:

- Clearly knowing and referring all results to my end goal.
- Tracking exactly where my leads are coming from.
- Tracking my conversion for each lead source.
- Honing in on the best source of conversion.
- Examining what I can do to increase conversions in slow sources.
- Repeating the process consistently.

Obviously this is a very simplified version of what the process would look like, but it should paint the picture of just how important keeping score is.

Keeping score also helps us in the short-term as well as the long-term. This is where our self-esteem bank account comes into play.

Imagine having a bank account. This bank account is special. It determines our ability to act in unison with our goals. Self-esteem can be defined as a feeling of pride in yourself. Alternately, it can be defined as the promises you make to yourself and keep.

Self Esteem > Estimation > Value > Trust

So self-esteem is how much trust you have in yourself. Every time you achieve a goal, no matter how great or small, you get a little hit of dopamine. When this happens, your self-esteem bank account gets a deposit. When you don't achieve your goals, your bank account gets a withdrawal. By keeping score of all of these little deposits and withdrawals, you'll be able to determine how much is in your self-esteem bank account.

The more you have deposited, the easier it is for you to achieve; the less there is, the harder. Pretty simple, right?

Now I'm not suggesting you document every single thing you do so you can keep track of your self-esteem bank account. You can, but you don't have to. Just being aware of this notion should help you. One exercise that I do every night and that may serve you is answering this question:

What three things can I be grateful for that I accomplished today and bring me closer to my goal?

You might have noticed that the question is loaded. This is because you're focusing on:

- More than one thing.
- The positives rather than the negatives.
- Things related to bringing you closer to achieving your goal.

On the days where you seemingly have an absolute nightmare, I bet you can at least think of three things you can be grateful for. Repeating this exercise every night is a great way of keeping score while serving to boost your self-esteem bank account.

You're depositing three things into your self-esteem bank account every night, and trust me, these add up – which in turn provides you with more trust in yourself, which provides you with the confidence to do what you need to do.

This covers keeping score. The next step is to identify the support you may need.

6. **Decide on Your Support**

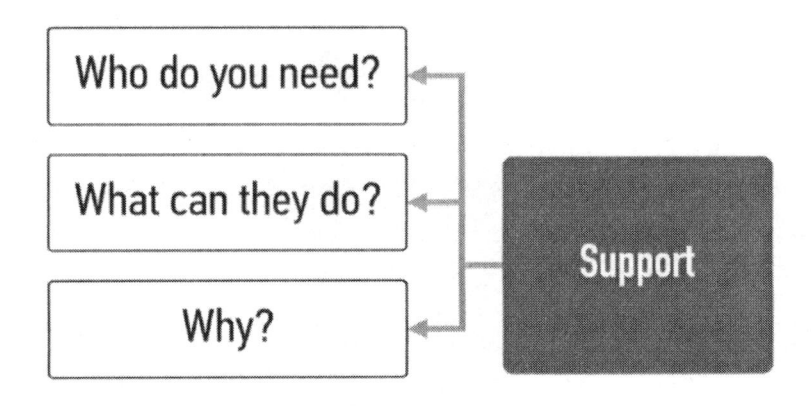

This step of the process can arguably accelerate your success more than any other. On top of that, it can also accelerate your ability to go through the other steps. I kept this step last because of its importance.

Having support along your journey of change and achievement is essential in my book. Going it alone can be quite difficult. It can leave you with a feeling of isolation. The feeling of being on an island. This is especially true when you're running a business.

> In fact my GKIC monthly marketing and business building summit is designed to provide all of these benefits and more. You do not have to wait until you finish this book to join, visit www.JohnMulry.com/GKIC now to find out how you can align yourself and your business with exactly who and what you need to succeed.

Defining your support structure comes from answering some simple yet powerful questions:

- Who do you need to support you?
- Why do you need them?
- What can they do for you?

These questions can be answered in one fell swoop. It all starts with who you align yourself with and who you distance yourself from. Let's start with who you align yourself with.

- 20 -

Three Kinds of People

"I've learned that people will forget what you said, people will forget what you did, but people will never forget how you made them feel."

–Maya Angelou

The people you surround yourself with not only can but *will* have a profound effect on your level of success, whether in regard to your health and fitness, your business or career, your dreams, and your life goals.

You're probably aware that I'm a believer that if you want to improve yourself you've got to surround yourself with the people, resources, and tools that will best serve you. For example, people who have either achieved what you want to achieve, are willing to help you, or want to achieve something similar.

It's one of the main reasons I'm constantly reading, striving to improve, and going to the best personal development courses, events, and seminars. It's accountability 101 – surround yourself with like-minded people and you can't help but be inspired, right?

Let me illustrate with the help of a story. I want you to vividly imagine each detail of this story so you can actually *feel* what's going on. Try and relate it to yourself. For this example, we'll use Bob again.

Bob has made the decision to take action and finally change his business. He sets himself a goal of growing his customer base, generating more revenue, more often, from his clients and taking charge of his business once and for all. He's sick and tired of waking up every morning and literally feeling disgusted by his business. He feels awful throughout the day because he doesn't have the belief to do anything, he wakes up every morning feeling worse than he did when he went to bed, and he dreads each day as it comes. He struggles to do what most would consider easy things: getting up, going to work, marketing consistently, even helping his kids with their homework, or playing with them in the evenings.

All these "simple" things are a constant battle for him, so one morning, he decides he's had enough and commits to changing. When he gets frustrated, he turns to drink – he feels it's the only comfort he has, the only solace he can find, but afterwards he inevitably feels even more disgusting and the cycle repeats over and over. He finally decides that he's going to take action and take control back again.

This is a big step for Bob, but there's one problem – he's on an island. Not in the literal sense, but in the sense that all his life he's been around "yes" people who have become accustomed to the way Bob's life has unfolded and never really thought about whether or not he wanted to change.

Sure they'd encourage him if he started something new, but when he'd fail he'd be "comforted" by comments like, "It's fine," "Your business is grand the way it is," and, "Why do you want to change, anyway?" While this was briefly comforting to Bob, it wasn't actually helping him. It was short-term comfort but would eventually pull him back into the rut he so badly wanted to get out of.

Your Elephant's Under Threat

So what's the point of this story? It's pretty simple, actually, and something that's often overlooked. It's pretty hard to try and achieve something on your own; being on an island is lonely as hell. But the great thing is that there's absolutely no reason to be on this island.

Take my own goals for the Expect Success Academy – even though I'm a pretty darn ambitious person and have more than enough drive to achieve my goals – it's going to be hard as hell to try and achieve them on my own.

By going to the seminars, courses, and mastermind events, having a coach, and reading books, partnering with GKIC, I'm surrounding myself with three kinds of people:

1. People who HAVE achieved what I want to achieve.

2. People who WANT to achieve what I want to achieve.

3. People who are willing to HELP me achieve my goals.

When you surround yourself with any of these types of people (the more the better), you're not only giving yourself a great chance of succeeding, but you're giving yourself the *best* chance of succeeding.

These people are not too far from you: friends, family members, a coach, a mentor. Beyond this you could look at online communities and support groups – you'd be amazed how many like-minded people you'll find if you open up and look for them.

Beyond that you can find your inspiration in books, articles, and blogs. Everything helps. They're called "force multipliers." You're attacking your goals from all angles, not just one – you have multiple poles in the water, so to speak. Now given this, let's revisit Bob's story.

It's the exact same scenario, but this time he's surrounded himself with these kinds of people. He has also gone through the process of defining exactly what he wants and has clearly defined the rules.

Bob creates an environment that will enable him and *he* decides on his support structure. He enlists the help of a coach and joins a monthly marketing and business building summit. His coach is committed to helping him achieve his goal; he introduces him to people who have achieved his goal already and provides him with a community framework that puts him in contact with others that are looking to achieve the same type of goal he is. Now, does he have a better or worse chance of succeeding?

How many times have you set out to achieve something but gone it alone? Or alternately, how many times have you been held back because you had the wrong types of people around you?

Here are those three questions again:

- Who do you need to support you?
- Why do you need them?
- What can they do for you?

These questions are great, but because it's you who defines them, you also get to define what happens if they don't meet your expectations or the people in your current support structure don't meet your needs.

- What if they don't do what you expect of them?
- What if they hold you back? In other words, what if they become a threat?
- How will they be fired?

This may be a hard truth to swallow. Not everyone wants to see you succeed. Not everyone wants to see you be the best you can be. There are people out there, for one reason or another, who are like energy vampires. They suck the life and our ability to achieve out of us, oftentimes unintentionally. The harshest thing about this truth is that sometimes it can be our friends or family that are the ones holding us back.

Before I discovered the massive impact that threats can have on my life, I would've written that we need to 'fire' those energy vampires. We should minimise our contact with these energy vampires and surround ourselves with people who will support us in our quest for change or achievement.

It comes back to the expect success cycle we discussed earlier. The input we allow into our lives influences our ability to think, act, and ultimately, succeed. If the only people we have around us are these so-called energy vampires, then the input we are receiving is all negative, thus our chances for success is minimal.

The thing is, though, the energy vampires in our lives are themselves under threat for one reason or another. For this reason, the word 'fire' seems harsh, especially if they are close friends or loved ones. Once you have gone through the process of identifying your own threat and overcoming it through the framework I have discussed in this book, you may find that you will be a lot more empathetic to others around you.

This was a big wake up call for me when I realised it. I was going over my notes on my flight back from my Mindmap coaching certification training and it struck me. Before the course, I was 100% adamant that I needed to distance myself from those people who brought me down, held me back, or were just negative by nature. That's what I thought they were, anyway: negative by nature.

And this served me well; I was creating my own environment that would enable me to achieve my own goals. In the gym, I care little for small talk. I prefer to train alone and listen to audiobooks (at 2x speed) while I work out. This minimised my exposure to the noise and nonsense that's rampant in gyms while maxiising my learning and time maximisation potential. My results from doing so speak for themselves.

In my social circles, I've distanced myself from naysayers and negative influences because they weren't in line with my purpose. From a gossip and news point of view, I avoid it altogether, occasionally reading business news or sports news. This way I'm not subjected to the media and constant negativity in the press. This one is quite funny, considering my girlfriend is a journalist and editor (and a fantastic one at that).

Limiting negative influences and energy vampires has served me well, but on the plane back from the course I started thinking about all the people in my life who I considered a negative influence, some of whom were friends, sometimes even family. Now my thought process had switched. I was no longer labelling them as negative.

Then it was about figuring out *why* they were negative. The answer was staring me in the face. They were under threat in some area of their lives. This was a big *Aha!* moment for me as I can show empathy and compassion when someone is negative now instead of just labelling them and forcing them out of my life.

It's funny, I was on the plane and I could see negativity all around me, but this time I started searching for elements that would give me an inclination of what their threat might be. It was empowering, inspiring, and extremely motivating.

This is important. Yes, I do suggest you limit your exposure to negative people, but do so under the realisation that the person isn't inherently negative; they, too, are under threat, and showing some empathy towards them and their feelings might just be what they need to see the positive in things.

When you have your support structure defined and have set up some criteria that you would like them to abide by (through the questions we explored), you will have everything you need to overcome your threat and completely change any area of your life from personal, business, health, and wellness to professional.

John Mulry, MSc

– 21 –

Bringing Everything Together

"An unexamined life is not worth living."

–Socrates

If you look back over the stages, you should start to see that each of these elements are linked, and when you start the process, everything starts to come together quite quickly.

The steps we went through were:

- Define the goal or endgame
- Create, understand, and play by your rules
- Create the environment
- Keep score
- Support

Each step is determined by you, and each step is interlinked. Once you start to go through each step, it will become clear what the next steps are. That's the power of answering the right questions.

Now, I can completely understand that the 30,000-foot advanced view of my system can be really daunting and overwhelming at first.

It doesn't have to be… the core behind it is simple:

- Define what you want
- Refine what it's not

- Align with what is going to bring you there

What makes it so powerful is the flexibility, individuality, and simplicity it affords you.

The beauty of it is that when you Define, Refine, and Align, you start to figure out everything and the solution that's unique *to you* will present itself. That's one of the biggest takeaways from this, *unique to you and your situation*. Everyone is different, every problem is different, and each situation calls for different approaches. Sure, we may share some characteristics in our problems, but the individual that bears those problems is unlike any other.

Another realisation from following this model is that the strategies and solutions you need will unfold in front of you as you need them. The systems, tools, and resources you then use are only limited by your imagination – and your willingness to try different things. They are means to an end.

As long as they help you succeed and you enjoy the process, who cares?

This is where the process really shines: you won't be doing things because someone told you to or because it was another shiny object that came your way and caught your eye; you'll be following a plan that *you* defined, *you* refined, and that's aligned with everything *you* need to succeed.

– 22 –

Doing it Alone

"The best time to plant a tree was 20 years ago. The second best time is now."

–Chinese Proverb

Going through theses steps yourself will reveal a lot. You will start to understand what was holding you back from achieving, from changing, and from progressing. One caveat with this model is *you*. What I mean is that your ability and willingness (or lack thereof) to ask yourself and answer some testing questions may hold you back.

You most certainly can succeed on your own by following this model, but the beauty of it is that you don't have to. Sometimes when you go it alone, it's easier to avoid the real testing questions. This is because you're essentially acting as a player *and* a coach.

We can look at this through an example of two football teams. On the one hand you have a football team where the manager of the football team is also one of the star players. He's the player/coach. The example that comes to mind for me here is that of Luis Amor Rodriguez of Harchester United from the short-lived TV series *Dream Team*.

Being both the star player and the coach is not only demanding, it can be counterintuitive, too. When you're on the field playing, it's very hard for you to see the full picture. As the saying goes, you can't see the forest for the trees.

This is because you can easily get caught up in playing the game instead of managing or overseeing the game. A great football manager knows when to make changes and knows how to assemble a team that will win. If you're stuck on the field playing the whole time, it's very difficult to know when to change things and even more difficult to win.

Now compare that to a team that has a dedicated coach. The coach here is on the sidelines and can see exactly what's going right while pinpointing the areas that need addressing. He can see what the players can't see. He has the ability to see problems with the 30,000-foot perspective.

Given these examples, can you see how going through this process alone may seem like you're acting as both the star player and coach? You may get results but you won't be as effective, as strong, or as successful as you would be if you had a dedicated coach.

Are you currently a player/coach in your life or in your business? Wouldn't you agree that having a coach, someone who is impartial and will ask you the questions you need to answer, would benefit you in overcoming your threat and achieving your goals?

This is what the power of coaching affords you.

– 23 –

The Power of Coaching

"The way to get started is to quit talking and begin doing."

–Walt Disney

The simplest and best definition of a coach is that a coach helps you win. That is my aim for the Expect Success Academy: to help you win. Having a coach has a number of benefits:

- Asks you the tough questions
- Helps you define your game
- Helps you create and define your rules for the game
- Helps you create the environment
- Keeps score and holds you accountable
- Offers the support you need
- Sees what you cannot see
- Reveals you to yourself
- Helps you find your truth
- Acts as a mirror

With the Expect Success Academy, I aim to be right at the source of the problem. Imagine a factory dumping waste material into a river. Trying to drain the waste material five kilometres downstream isn't going to solve to the problem. You need to hit the source. The Expect Success Academy aims to arrive at the source (the factory) to find and solve the problem right where it begins.

All of that sounds great, yet there seems to be a stigma around coaching. There are a few myths about coaching that I would like to address. Here a five of them.

Myth #1 – Coaching is soft.

This isn't true. Coaching can sometimes be perceived as being 'woo-woo' and very light-hearted. Nothing could be further from the truth. Coaching is hard because it requires truth and trust. It requires you to answer some tough questions about yourself, your business, and your future.

Myth #2 – Coaching is slow.

The reality is that nothing is faster than coaching. Coaching requires truth, and there is nothing more powerful than the truth. When you reveal the truth, you'll know exactly what needs to be done and can act immediately. One hour of coaching can reveal more truth than a lifetime of guessing.

Myth #3 – Coaching is difficult.

Coaching isn't difficult; it does require you to answer some testing questions that will reveal a lot about yourself. That in itself is empowering, not difficult. The process is quite simple, too; a great coach will elicit the answers from you, not provide them for you.

Myth #4 – Coaching cannot be measured.

Coaching can be measured directly in a number of different ways. It can be measured by your action, self-esteem, and arriving at your required solution.

Myth #5 – Coaching creates dependence.

This is another myth. Coaching doesn't create dependence; on the contrary. It creates interdependence because you come for answers. This happens when the questions which draw out answers you already have but can't find are asked.

Not only is coaching designed to help you win, it helps you evolve. The whole coaching process as well as the Define, Refine, and Align model that ESA is built around is designed so that you can continuously evolve.

The model for change that I described in detail brings you through a process of evolution naturally by way of design.

It starts with your problem. Through coaching, we extract what needs to be done. We then work on the new behaviours that are needed. When conflict and problems arise (they are a good thing), we then define, refine, and align again to arrive at a resolution. The next stage after resolution is integration, which brings about evolution.

Once you have integrated the resolution, you've overcome your threat and know you can celebrate that success and aim to grow further. It's more of a spiral than a cycle because how far you go is limited only by your imagination. That is how you win continuously.

- Problem
- Extraction
- New Behaviours
- Overcome Conflict
- Resolution
- Integration
- Evolution

John Mulry, MSc

– 24 –

What Can the Expect Success Academy Do for You?

"Nothing is impossible, the word itself says, 'I'm possible!'"

–Audrey Hepburn

This is essentially my aim for the Expect Success Academy, helping you win and evolve. To help you dig down and uncover the greatness you have inside of you. The ESA coaching approach is two-fold: it's a combination of coaching and strategy.

First we go through the coaching process, as described. Then, once we have all the answers we need, we build strategy and solutions into the equation so you have a clear path to follow. The beauty here is that you will have a defined plan of action for implementing the many ideas we will discover throughout the coaching process. For me, both parts are essential. Coaching without strategy leaves you with loads of ideas, inspiration, and motivation without direction, structure, or implementation.

Strategy without coaching gives you structure, direction, and implementation without defining, refining, and aligning with what you really want and need.

At the Expect Success Academy, I have five modes of development that I use and will continue to use.

- Information Products
- Seminars/Speaking

- GKIC Local Chapter Private Membership Meeting
- Coaching
- Masterminding

Information Products

The first mode of development is through information. Through information products you will be able to start the process at a level that you are comfortable with. This book is an example of this. It's an information product that serves to show you why it is you cannot change or achieve and what you can do about it. Typically, these are entry-level products and offer a lot of value and information on 'how to' and the steps you need to take. Generally, they are not backed up with accountability.

The age we live in makes information abundant. This is fantastic and we are blessed to live in such an age, but we must take caution for three reasons.

The first is that we must be aware of the idea of information overload, or paralysis by analysis. I described earlier that this was something that I fell victim to for years. I wanted more and more information but never acted upon any of the information I obtained. Remember, knowledge that isn't applied is essentially worthless; we must have a framework for applying the knowledge that we obtain.

The second reason is that there is an awful lot of noise, misinformation, hype, and nonsense out there today in this information age. This can make deciphering what is useful from what is not really confusing. You must have a framework for defining rules and creating an environment that makes it easier for you to align with the information you need, information that will serve you.

The third and final reason is a little bit tricky. There is an awful lot of information out there and an awful lot of that information is free. This again is fantastic, but therein lies the problem.

When we get something for free, it has no perceived value. It doesn't matter if the information contained has the potential to completely change our lives; if we don't perceive it as being valuable, we won't use it.

If it's a free book, we won't read it and implement what we learn. If it's a free course, we won't follow through and complete it. If it's free training or free coaching, we mightn't go into it willing to fully reveal the truth and with full commitment.

I know this first-hand from both sides of the coin. I have tonnes of resources, books, courses, and manuals that I have received for free, have gotten online for free, or subscribed to, and I have never used them. Now, the information in some of them is fantastic, but because they were free, they have no perceived value.

On the other hand, all of the courses, seminars, books, and masterminding events I have attended came with an investment of time and money. Because of that, I am more likely to act on and implement what I learn.

Anything that comes with an investment, whether that's an investment of money, resources, or time, will always have a higher perceived value than something that's free with no element of accountability.

Similarly, I have fallen victim to this. I have given away courses, books, seminars, workshops, coaching, and training in my business at various different levels, and without question, the participation, attendance, implementation, completion, and commitment has been lower while the absenteeism, objection, and wastefulness has been higher.

Something you pay for will always get your attention more than something you got for free. Take this book, for example. If you've paid for it, you're more likely to read it (and apply what you learn) because you've invested money in it.

The investment isn't always monetary, though. Take bartering, for example. One of my coaches, David Keane of Progressive Living who I meet once a week is a mutually beneficial agreement whereby he coaches me and I coach him. Now, no money changes hands but there is an exchange of coaching, so it is not free. Trust me; my value perception of David's coaching is very high.

The lesson here is that yes, there is a lot of free information available, but until you have made an investment in acquiring and implementing that information, it's less likely you will use said information. I'm not completely discounting the wealth and value of the free information that's out there, I just want to be clear about how we perceive that value.

Some questions that will help you here are:

- How many books have you downloaded for free and actually read and acted upon?
- How many free seminars or workshops have you signed up for but never attended?
- How many times have you dismissed something because it was free?
- How many times have you invested a lot of money into a course, book, seminar, or event and *not* attended?
- Which has the higher perceived value, something you pay for or something you get for free?

Seminars/Speaking

Through seminars and speaking I get to spread the Expect Success Academy message to a wider audience. Having been invited as a guest speaker and seminar leader for organisations and businesses such as JCI Galway (Junior Chamber of Commerce), the Ballybane Enterprise Centre and Online Marketing in Galway, I know I can positively impact groups as well as individuals. This wider audience plays a big role in your development, too. Remember we talked about the need to create your environment. In that environment, we need to align ourselves with the right types of people. Seminars are a perfect example of this.

I remember the first big seminar I went to. It was called Fitness Business Summit and it was in California. It was organised by one of my first mentors, fitness business and marketing expert Bedros Keuilian. It was a two-day event in Orange County. I flew all the way over especially, just to meet Bedros and Jay Abraham. Actually, a few weeks prior to the event I appeared on the radio with Jay where he and Brian Tracy dissected my business. When your on live on air with these guys, you better use your two ears more than your one mouth.

Another major event which I have already mentioned was the one I attended in Texas. I got to work closely with Dave Dee, Darcy Juarez and the other like minded entrepreneurs. Those few days were amazing, again proof that I was in the right place with the right people. I was the only one there from Ireland and I started to realise that maybe I should do something about it. Maybe I should be the one to bring GKIC style marketing to Ireland. A year later that's what I'm doing now through the Expect Success Academy.

When I got backfrom Texas I implemented what I had learned and started putting things in place... by taking massive action. I invested, I consumed everything I got and get and most importantly I take *massive* action on what I consume.

Because of my willingness to get out of my comfort zone and attend these seminars and events (regardless of how far or for how much) I opened up new opportunities for myself and my business. I've been handpicked by Dan Kennedy and GKIC to be Ireland's first GKIC Certified Business Advisor where I show other businesses in Ireland that they too can prosper through investing, consuming and acting with GKIC and 'Dan Kennedy' style direct response marketing.

The people I met and meet at these events tick the boxes of the three who I needed and need to succeed.

They had achieved what I wanted to achieve, they were willing to help me achieve it, and they wanted the same things as I did. You get to form relationships and alliances with people who will bring you further than you can ever go on your own.

That's the beauty of seminars and speaking and that's why I aim to make them a big part of the Expect Success Academy.

Not only are you getting the benefits of an expert willing to show you how to overcome threat and change, but you are also getting the opportunity to surround yourself with the exact kinds of people you need to succeed.

GKIC Local Chapter Private Membership Meeting

As mentioned, Dan Kennedy, who is a serial entrepreneur, multimillionaire, author of over 18 business books, and widely regarded as one of the the top marketing minds in the world, hand picked and trained me to be his guy in Ireland.

> The local GKIC chapter in Galway is an exciting networking, idea-sharing, and business building support group unlike ANY other. It's a hybrid, combining a mastermind meeting with smart people coaching each other, a networking meeting with ambitious business owners helping each other, a strategy-rich and successful example-laden mini-seminar with great presentations, recognition of your creativity, and achievements from people who "get it," all under my direction, bearing my unique brushstrokes.
>
> Visit www.JohnMulry.com/GKIC if you are interested in joining this fascinating group.

Coaching

Coaching, as I've already described, is designed for one purpose: to help you win. Having outlined the power of coaching and its immense effectiveness, I hope you can realise why it's one of the pillars of my academy. Coaching with the Expect Success Academy is by application only and can be done in many forms, depending on the individual, the business, their location, and resources available.

Masterminding

What is a mastermind? Well, I think the best definition doesn't come from me but from Napoleon Hill, who, in my mind (and many others'), has changed the world more than any other man before him. If you have yet to read Napoleon Hill's *Think and Grow Rich* at this stage of your life, I urge you to do so. You're doing yourself and your business a disservice if you do not. I bring my copy of TAGR with me everywhere. He defines it as:

"The coordination of knowledge and effort of two or more people who work toward a definite purpose in the spirit of harmony."

He continues:

"No two minds ever come together without thereby creating a third, invisible, intangible force, which may be likened to a third mind [the mastermind]."

To give you an overview of what a mastermind is, let's put into practice the exercise of 'untying the nots' and define what a mastermind is not.

It's not a course:

Members of a mastermind may agree to invite in guest speakers and teachers occasionally; however, a mastermind is not a course, a class, or schooling. The core focus is brainstorming, accountability, and support.

It's not group coaching:

Mastermind groups are not about me as the facilitator coaching you. They're about the members working together, sharing with each other to work towards achieving definitive goals.

It's not a networking group:

While the opportunity to work collaboratively with each other, share leads, and explore possible joint ventures will likely occur, this is not the main focus.

The Expect Success Academy mastermind is based around its members. Commitment is key. You will provide and be given feedback, brainstorm new ideas and solutions, and maintain accountability structures that serve to keep you focused and on track. It's a supportive community of colleagues working together to move each other to new levels. It aims to help you win and evolve.

Think of it like having a board of directors, coaching, and a peer advisory group all rolled into one, providing you with the rules, environment, accountability, and support you need to reach new levels in business and in life. Again, masterminding with the Expect Success Academy is by application only as the success of a mastermind comes down to members' commitment moreso than anything else.

- 25 -

Need Additional Help?

"Tell me and I forget. Teach me and I remember. Involve me and I learn."

– Benjamin Franklin

This can be the end, or the beginning. If you made it this far and you have read all the way through, you should count yourself in the top percentile. Making the decision to read this book was the first action step. Actually following through with reading it was the next.

As I have mentioned, information received, whether it's from physical books, eBooks, seminars, videos, audios, courses, or from person-to-person interaction, is nigh on useless unless it's acted upon. You got this far and for that you should be applauded.

The next step for you is to take action and implement what you have learned in this book. Some of this information may have been new for you and some you may have come across before; that doesn't matter. What matters is whether or not you actively apply it to your life, your business, your dreams, and your aspirations.

I wanted to have this book laid out as more of an actionable workbook than anything else, and please know, I want to challenge you.

Too often in the past, I would read a book and get really excited about the information, my enthusiasm would grow and

I'd get a burst of motivation. Then life would get in the way and I'd soon forget about the book and forget about what I had read and learned. Has this happened to you before? My challenge to you now is to follow through with the frameworks and methodologies I've presented to you and act upon them.

Identify which areas of your life or business are threatening you. Then, through the step by step plan I've given you, overcome them so you can achieve whatever you want. I want you to be aware that this will not be an easy task, but *you can do it*.

If you value the information I have presented to you, if you found it interesting and engaging then, I promise you there's a lot more where that came from. The Expect Success Academy's primary mission is to help you achieve, help you win.

I know my systems, strategies, and solutions can transform your business and your life. It certainly has transformed mine as well as many others' whom I've I helped in the past and coach now. I think virtually anyone could benefit from this kind of coaching, anyone who's struggling to see the forest for the trees in their business, who's disillusioned by the sheer amount of pressure of running a business. The business owner who's struggling to generate new leads and clients can benefit from it. But also, anyone whose company is thriving and they're feeling bored or uninspired by it all. Or any business owner who is feeling lost, alone, and 'on an island.'

Imagine what the Expect Success Academy can do for you and your business.

Still, it isn't for everybody. You have to want explosive growth and you need to be honest enough to answer some testing questions, which, if answered openly, could transform your business and life overnight.

But you don't need to answer them and do it alone. I'll help you with that. Through my five modes of development, I can provide the materials and regular coaching to help you reach and fulfil your potential (in a way that's enjoyable). And you'll be amazed at what you can do with your sudden, newfound ability to deal with everything that comes your way.

I'm not looking to pressure you into requesting more information or availing of my products, coaching, and/or consulting. In fact, I've decided to be pretty picky about whom I work with. You have to apply and not all applications are accepted. I want to ensure the people I work with are committed to getting results.

> But because you're reading this book, I can assume that you're looking for more from your life and business than you currently have, and if you let me, I can show you how to get it. If you've ever asked yourself, *"What is the one thing I can do to change the scale and success of my life and business right now?"* This is it.
>
> If this sounds like you then visit:
>
> www.JohnMulry.com

John Mulry, MSc

– 26 –

Resources

"If we knew what it was we were doing, it would not be called research, would it?"

– Albert Einstein

Throughout this book I have mentioned a number of people, books, and courses that have had a positive effect on my journey. Below you will find a list of what I believe is essential reading/listening:

Think and Grow Rich by Napoleon Hill

Personal Power II by Tony Robbins

The Go Giver by Bob Burg and John David Mann

Psycho-Cybernetics by Dr. Maxwell Maltz

Audacity of Success by Brian Grasso

Ready Fire Aim by Michael Masterson

The E-Myth Revisited by Michael E. Gerber

Anything and everything by Dan Kennedy.

www.JohnMulry.com/dan

In the following section you will find details on how you can get access to the full-size define, refine, and align illustrations in this book, along with business building worksheets and downloadable MP3 audios of the three bonus interviews with Paul Chubbuck, Dax Moy, and Brian Grasso.

On page 225 you will also find 'The Missing Chapter,' which was especially written for small business owners and entrepreneurs.

– 27 –

Bonus Downloads

"Leadership and learning are indispensable to each other."

– John F. Kennedy

Visit www.JohnMulry.com/book-bonus to get instant access to the following bonuses:

- MP3 downloads of the three bonus interviews.
- Full-size PDF downloads of all of the Define, Refine, and Align illustrations and diagrams.
- Future updates and access to the "Your Elephant's Under Threat" workbook.
- The Define, Refine, and Align Checklist.
- "Is your business really a business?" in-depth questionnaire.
- €466 worth of pure business-building and money-making information

To get access to these bonuses visit www.JohnMulry.com/book-bonus

The following pages contain three bonus interviews that I conducted while researching for this book. The interviews are with trauma therapy expert Paul Chubbuck of Releasing the Past, coach and mentor of mine Dax Moy, and author of *Audacity of Success* Brian Grasso.

John Mulry, MSc

– 28 –

Bonus Interview with Paul Chubbuck

Who is Paul Chubbuck?

John: John Mulry here from the Expect Success Academy. I would like to welcome you to this very special call. This call today is exclusively for my book, *Your Elephant's Under Threat*. When I was researching the book and looking into the background and methodologies that I presented there, I sought out the best resources and experts.

One of those experts I have with me today: Paul Chubbuck. I will tell you a small bit about Paul now, and then we can get started on the actual interview itself. Many years ago, Paul found himself in a painful, repeating pattern of heartbreak and emotional hurt. It was never what he wanted or intended, but it kept happening anyway.

When he experienced too much pain, he started earnestly looking for answers in any reasonable place — self-help books, 12-step programs, therapy, mentors, mythology, poetry, and spirituality. Paul found out that a lot of these answers were helpful, but the work that helped him transform his life the most, quit getting emotionally hurt, and quit hurting others, was Somatic Experiencing. This is the work that he now offers to others. Paul has a Masters in Counseling and is a certified Somatic Experiencing Practitioner (SEP), with additional certification to teach Somatic Trauma Resolution (STR), both of which are powerfully effective in the treatment of abuse, loss, injury, and other trauma.

His 35-year professional and personal growth path — seeking and finding solutions to his own challenges — forms the foundation for what he offers to others. Paul's expertise lies in the compassionate and skilled way he helps his clients rediscover the joy and excitement in their inherent self-healing abilities. Paul, I am thrilled to have you on this call and contributing to my book, *Your Elephant's Under Threat*.

Paul: Thank you, John. Nice to meet you.

Methodologies of Releasing the Past

John: I have some great questions for Paul, so we will get straight into it. So the first question is, how did you first get into the methodologies you teach through Releasing the Past?

Paul: Well, as you suggested in your introduction, I had my own challenges. I think when we are in our 20s, we can coast on the expectations that all that's needed to find happiness is that we meet the right lover and get the right job. But when we fall flat on our faces a few times, then that gets called into question. For me that happened around age 30 and I started seeking a little deeper.

What I recognised was that one of the problems I had was a difficulty in simply being present with myself, with my own body, with my own feelings, with my own sensations, and with other people. I got very curious about this phenomenon of distracting, avoiding, denying, and dissociating from my own experience. I also recognised that other people did this, too. It was not just my problem.

So, for a long time, I had a lot of questions about this and it kind of drove my seeking to find answers to various spiritual paths and personal growth experiences that began to address that over time. As you suggested in your introduction, the Somatic Experience that I eventually discovered approximately a dozen years ago was kind of a culmination for me that brought a lot of different things under one umbrella and helped me understand it all better.

What Does "Releasing the Past" Mean?

John: Okay. Just kind of touching upon your website and business, Releasing the Past. If you were to define "releasing the past," how would you put it?

Paul: Well, the past in this case refers to our most challenging experiences in life that tend to bring about the so-called fight-or-flight response, the survival response, the instinctual part of our brain that only cares about our heart continuing to beat and how this gets triggered.

Especially as a child, this gets triggered in many situations that seem to be threatening or where love is denied, the child is neglected or left alone, or where there is abuse of any kind: sexual, emotional, or spiritual. So, when that gets triggered and where there is not much support or protection around for that child or young person, it tends to get ingrained as a survival pattern. That may indeed help the child survive emotionally or even physically. 20 years later, it may not be so pretty. It may not be so functional. That's where the problems come in. When you reach, as I suggested in my case around 30 or even 40 or 50, and you say, "*How come my relationships are not working? How come I cannot get the kind of job or career that I desire?*" Usually, the answer is these old and ingrained trauma patterns that helped us once but are not working anymore.

John: Very good.

Paul: So, that's the past. Releasing it, well, that kind of speaks for itself; it has to do with the process of investigating and the feeling of releasing the anxiety that is embedded in our bodies and nervous systems so that we can have more choice.

Tips for Troubled People

John: Brilliant! So, for people who are having trouble letting go of the past, what are your tips for them?

Paul: Well, I would say first of all, go easy on yourself. It was really important to me to quit looking at these ingrained old patterns as being problems, as being bad, as feeling shame around, and to actually recognise that they were part of my brilliant survival strategies. I mean, for a child, for example, at age four. I am just giving an example here. It's not really a personal example. It's from a client. I remember a client told me that they could tell by the sound of the father's tires on the gravel driveway outside whether he had been drinking and was angry or not. Therefore, what they needed to do was run for cover in a room and hide. So to be that brilliant, to be that sensitive to your environment, and to know how to take care of yourself at age four, that is incredible. Now, at age 34, to be that kind of scared, anxious, paranoid, and over-sensitive to sounds could be a problem. You see what I mean?

Paul: So, it's important for this person who may be listening to this interview to realise that the problems in your life today can engender a kind of self-respect that may have been only shame before. That is the beginning of change, to realise that you are not a bad person, you are not just an addict, you are not just a dysfunctional person. You are a survivor. There's nobility in that.

Biggest Misconceptions

John: Very good. So then, from your experience, what are the common misconceptions when it comes to trauma therapy in which you specialise?

Paul: Probably the biggest one is the fear that in order to heal it, a person must relive it and thus feel a fearsome amount of anxiety that seems totally daunting at any age. This is really a misconception. We find instead that a much more productive approach is to help a person build resources. Resources mean anything in a person's life which helps them feel empowered, successful, or joyful.

John: Okay.

Paul: This is not just an intellectual concept. It's not just a memory. What I am interested in is helping a client find something like this, maybe when 20 years ago they used to love dance and now when they tell me that they love to dance, something happens in their body and they pay attention to it: some relaxation, some slowing of the breath, some tingling, some release of adrenaline. That's where the resource has the transforming power. That's where it really becomes a part of the healing process.

John: Okay. Are there any other common misconceptions?

Paul: Well, I think the one that I wanted to focus on there was that people think that they have to relive the trauma to heal it. What I am suggesting is that it's not true. There are better ways that have to do with a more positive approach to finding ways to like yourself, to respect yourself, to feel positive feelings in your body and your emotions. Sometimes people do need to talk about what happened. Therapy can be a good place for that. That is certainly something that I allow and invite when it's appropriate. It's just that if a person approaches the healing process thinking, "That is what I've got to do, and I do not want to go there because it is too darn scary," then that will put them off.

We are Limited by Our Past Trauma

John: Okay. So, what are your thoughts on the idea that our ability to change in a positive way is limited to how well we can overcome our past trauma?

Paul: Yeah. This is a very interesting question. If by overcoming our past trauma you or the person hearing this thinks of some kind of a willful endurance task, you know like a kind of knight in shining armor that has to pull out his lance and slay the dragon, if that is the image, that may be a problem. Because anybody who has had a challenging childhood or has otherwise been traumatised, basically the place where they are stuck is that they don't know how to overcome that past trauma.

John: Yeah.

Paul: And they don't know how to overcome it when they meet it face to face today. If that dragon walks through the door, they're probably going to have exactly the same paralysed fear reaction that they had when they were a child. So, in that sense, overcoming past trauma can be daunting or seem impossible. But I don't disagree with your statement. I do agree that our ability to change is related to our ability to overcome. What I favour is a recognition that the part of our brains where the trauma is stored is the primitive, reptilian brain.

And this reptilian brain does not communicate in words or in logic. An example of that would be a child who is scared of monsters in the closet. That's not a logical thing. You can turn on the lights. You can open the door. You can show the kid that there are no monsters in there and put them back to bed, and they're probably still going to be scared of monsters.

Because it's stored in the reptilian brain. It has no bearing of logic or words. So a metaphorical approach is better. Things that make a difference in that part of the brain are poetry, music, and soft speech that tends to slow the breathing down.

So these other modes of communication can touch that part of the brain and make that difference, and over time, a person who has... well, let me give you an example. Movies and stories like King Arthur, Harry Potter, Julia Roberts in Mona Lisa Smile, these can impact that primitive part of the brain because they are inspiration and they carry powerful images. Those are the healing content. Is this making sense?

John: It is. It makes perfect sense.

Paul: Okay. So I seek to help a person find the metaphors that will impact their deep psyche. The best of those metaphors come from the person themselves. I usually resist the urge to offer metaphors like I am in this conversation; I am suggesting, you know, King Arthur. That's a metaphor that *I* am offering. But in a therapy setting, I would say to the person something like, "What did you need at that moment when you felt so alone? If you could have had something that could have comforted you at age four when you were scared, what might that have looked like?" The unconscious is amazingly creative. It usually will indeed come up with a perfect metaphor if given time and space to do so.

John: That's really powerful, the way you described it there and the way that a reptilian brain does not react to words but reacts to metaphor. It paints a really good picture about how we need to deal with our trauma and so forth. Just touching on that a little bit more, because in your book *Releasing the Past*, you talked about the four keys of healing. Can you briefly discuss these here?

Four Keys to Healing

Paul: Sure. I touched on one already, resourcing. That's really core because in the beginning, resourcing is an image or a memory of something which helps you feel joyful, successful, or empowered. That's a short definition of resourcing. In practice, it usually refers to a memory of something good. You know, a place that you felt safe; a person whom you felt loving towards or loved by; a pet; an outdoor scene; a great spiritual teacher whom you felt close to. All of those are examples of possible resources, and these resources, when strongly remembered and felt in the body, will begin the process of releasing age old tensions and anxiety.

The second is what I call "presencing." What resource helps you feel a little safer, helps you slow down, helps you relax even a little bit? Then the possibility is there that you can become more present with yourself. That you can become curious about what's happening in your body. So, for example, you might slow down enough to notice that your breath is getting deeper. If you continue noticing, our minds are very quick. "Okay I got it, my breath went deeper, now what are we going to do next, Paul?" Ah, but that is only the beginning.

That is actually the first step, to notice the breath got a little deeper. Then I will say to my client, great. As your breath deepens, what else do you notice? The process continues. "Oh, I notice my feet are tingling. Now, my heart, I could feel my heart rate and it is slower." The process continues. I'll give you one quick example of the power of this. I had a client who really took this to heart and practiced it on her own at home as well as in the therapy sessions. She told me that after a few months, she no longer needed to go to the chiropractor because when she noticed a little creak in her neck and her back, she would just lay down and become fully present to her body. Her body would pop and adjust itself and she'd been following that for quite a while.

John: Wow.

Paul: So, that is what I mean by presencing. Reframing is the third of these four keys of releasing the past. When I, as a child, heard the phrase, "it's an ill wind that blows no good," I thought it was just saying that a bad wind does bad things. I did not understand the irony of the statement. What it is really saying is that we have to be a really ill wind for it to blow no good. Do you understand the difference and emphasis there?

John: Could you please explain it a little bit for the listeners?

Paul: In other words, the old cliché, "it's an ill wind that blows no good," is calling attention to the fact that even something that appears bad on the surface, an ill wind in this case, actually does good.

It brings rain where rain is needed. So, in that sense, reframing is a shift in perspective. The person who has suffered a lot, their lives have a tendency to be weary, suspicious, and fearful. Those qualities taken into one's life can cause one to look out constantly for the next bad thing that's coming in one's direction. Are you with me?

So when you are constantly on guard like that, your attention is focused on the next bad thing, the next feared thing. So, of course, such a person indeed notices all those bad or feared things. A part of the process is once you relax, once you become a little bit more present with yourself, then the reframing is a conscious choice to start looking outside that fear. A way that a person smiled at you, a way that a person was kind to you, a way that you drove through bad traffic and nothing bad happened, in fact people allowed you into the lane. You know what I'm saying? In other words, it is possible. It takes some effort because they have maybe decades of always looking for the next bad thing, but it's a habit that can profoundly change your life when you begin it. I would like to suggest to your listeners or readers a very simple exercise, if I may.

Keeping a Gratitude Journal

Paul: So this is pretty easy. I suggest that you find a friend to do this with, then two people will benefit and it will be support for you and help you actually follow through. But the exercise itself is very simple. You agree with this friend that you will each find three to five things each day that were really good in your life that day, things that you did, things that you noticed that were beautiful or wonderful or pleasant, or that you liked about yourself or what was happening to you that day. You relate these three things to the other person on the phone, by email, or in person, and while you are relating them, you become aware of what is happening inside your body. You will probably notice some positive experience, like your breath slowing, your heart opening. If you practice this each day for several weeks, which I suggest, or even a week, it will make a noticeable difference. You will almost undoubtedly notice a shift away from the frame where you may have this place of fear in life to one where you have an appreciation of life.

John: That's actually something I recommend my own clients do.

Paul: Yeah.

John: Just keep a gratitude journal.

Paul: Yes. It's the same thing, more or less.

John: I keep one myself, and I share it with my girlfriend. We share three things every night that we are grateful to each other for.

Paul: Wonderful!

John: You are absolutely right. It really does change your perspective. You start to appreciate a lot more things even if it appears that you have had a less-than-stellar day, you still have the chance to appreciate those two or three things that really did go well.

Paul: Yes.

John: That's a fantastic exercise and thank you for sharing it.

Paul: Yes. You are welcome. The fourth key is processing. It's a little bit hard to talk about it because in a way these steps build on each other. Processing, of these four, is the most sophisticated. It requires a little background or practice. But what I mean by processing is the willingness to stay on your feelings inside your own body in your challenges. Perhaps your girlfriend says something and you feel something in your body. You feel resentful or fearful. Now, what most people out there do at that point is strike out. They perceive, in this case the girlfriend, as being the cause of uncomfortable feelings; she shouldn't have done that, I'm going to let her know that's not okay. Or at the other extreme, you go into hiding. You just retreat, withdraw, and say, "That did not feel good. I am going to avoid this hurt." Both those are old, habitual trauma patterns and will not get us what we want in terms of relationships, in terms of intimacy, in terms of breakthrough, or in terms of personal healing. An example of what processing involves might be like this: if I was in an intimate relationship and that sort of thing happened and I am willing to stretch, I might say:

"Wow dear, I just noticed a big reaction in my body. Whew. I think I need to just sit down with this and feel what's happening. I obviously got really triggered by something you just said. Would you be willing to just be patient with me while I notice what's happening?"

This is, of course, a radically different approach if one does this, with or without the support of a loved one present. If you stay with these feelings, they will shift; they will move. There will be changes in your physical body experience, emotions will shift, and you will probably notice a growing insight as to where this came from and why you are acting this way. In any case, whether you get that insight or not, simply staying with the experience in the body will allow a release so that you don't feel so compelled to either withdraw or strike out.

John: Very good. Just that old way to describe that 4th key there. I think that one way I'm going to say it is that it's taking the time to slow everything down, especially in the age now that everything is fast and we react so fast, everything happens so fast.

Paul: Absolutely! Yeah. One of my teachers, Sharon Porter, likes to use the term taffy stretching, like you have seen in the carnivals, the machines that make sugar taffy.

They stretch the taffy repeatedly. So this image of taffy stretching says stretch it out, slow down this reaction. Let's slow that *way* down. What was happening to the body? What is happening? What's the word that triggered you? What was the meaning that you thought it had? Slow it way down. That is taffy stretching.

Top Questions

John: Very good. Just moving on to questions you get from your clients or from your subscribers. What would be the top three questions that you get and how do you answer them?

Paul: I think everybody that calls me has foremost on their mind, "Can you help me?" That, actually, is not voiced. It's implied by the phone call or the email. People, when they approach a helper, a coach, a therapist, they are in pain. They have so much pain that it got them to a point where they are willing to reach out to, usually, a stranger. When I think about it, that's a challenging thing – to kind of humble oneself and take the risk. So, "Can you help me?" is a big question. I am not so presumptuous as to simply answer that; I am not a salesman and don't say, *"Yes we can help you, let me just put you in the right automobile!"* It's such a sensitive topic. But what I do with people to help them decide if I can help them is that, as I walk them through somebody's processes, even in that first contact, I say, *"What is there in your life, or has there been in the past, that makes you feel joy or empowered or successful?"* Then, they start telling me about that. We are beginning to have a relationship.

So, that's one of the questions, "Can you help me?" Probably the second is, "How do you work with people?" How I work with people is to help them become more present to their sensations first. Because everybody can feel their sensations in their body, even if they are traumatised or dissociated. I help them find sensations that are pretty easy to feel, like can you feel the weight of your body in the chair? Can you feel the air passing over your hands or arms? This may be a stretch for some people because they have not been "in their bodies" for a while.

But even to feel these simple sensations will begin the process of slowing down, which we talked about a moment ago. This important process, it's slowing things down. So, how I work with people is through body awareness as an avenue to become more present with oneself. The third big question I get is, "How long will it take?" This is basically an impossible question but it's a very reasonable one for people to ask because they are also thinking about money, time, and impatience, too: getting out of pain as quickly as possible.

So, I try to address the underlying question as, "Can you help me get out of pain as quickly as possible?" Usually, the answer is yes. Because even a person in severe emotional pain will feel a lot less pain if they feel like somebody is giving them reasonable hope and some kind of connection and contact. That does not necessarily take a whole course of a year of therapy. That can happen in one simple session. Also, a person will gain hope if, for instance, they are able to come into their body in a way that is pleasant rather than scary. By that I am referring to a person who is highly traumatised and has left their body because it's too painful to be present in their body. There was too much heartache, there was too much bad memory going through their head where they dissociate or they suppress these feelings. So I try to help them find resources so they can remember what it was like to dance when they were a child or remember that camping trip three years ago where they had so much fun fishing and sitting by the lake. Then they start having thoughts like, "Oh, I'm not completely cut off from some sense of pleasure and joy in my life. I can still have some of these." That will bring hope, even though the permanent healing still takes longer.

John: Yeah. Those three questions and the way you have answered them are perfect. Thank you for sharing them.

Paul: You are welcome.

Understanding the Coaching Process

John: What would you say to someone who feels that they need to change and that they are stuck in certain areas of their life but they don't quite understand the power of coaching and the power that coaching can have?

Paul: Well, I am not quite sure how I will answer that. Let me see. Could you say it a little differently? Help me out here.

John: Okay. Let's say a client comes to you and starts to relay their thoughts and they feel that they need to change in a certain area of their life, whether there's a need to lose some weight or make some changes in their business or get over some past trauma, but then they don't quite understand the coaching process. What would you say to them?

Paul: Okay. I think I'm getting what you are saying. Well, there's kind of a tradition in our culture. I think it's a relatively recent one, of independence. "I don't really need help. I am fine." The cowboy hero riding off into the sunset, leaving his friends and lover behind, is kind of the classic image I draw on for this metaphor. The hero does not need anybody. We hope that in our cultural psyche and it cuts us off from the help we might otherwise get. I think this is so prevalent. I think that's what you are pointing to. Does that sound right? Is that where you are pointing at?

John: That's right. Yeah.

Paul: Okay. So there is a much older tradition which is really deep in our genes and our culture, but it's a little more hidden. Sometime before 100,000 years of this more recent independent, self-sufficient tradition, underneath that is a deep tradition of connection in community and mentorship, where elders spent time teaching young people and wisdom teachers shared the secrets of their traditions with the young people who showed promise in a given area or where a master craftsman showed the young apprentice how to make the shoes or do the carpentry. So this kind of tradition of connection in community and mentorship is truly ancient, going way back to when we were village and tribal people. Sometimes I call on these images which are present in our collective psyche to help people remember something more ancient that may fit for them and might help them open up to just the idea of having a teacher, having a valued helper.

John: Yeah. I definitely think the way you have explained that will really resonate with someone because we can all relate to that example, and everything we have ever learned, we learned from someone else.

Paul: Absolutely.

John: I think going through that process, especially the way you describe it there, would really, really help someone understand what the coaching process can be like. It's great that you shared that example. It even kind of meant more and solidifies my own experience. So, thanks very much for sharing that.

Paul: You are very welcome. Thanks for the question.

Get to Know More About Releasing the Past

John: So then, finally, I am kind of wrapping up everything here for anyone who's listening to this call, reads your interview, or what you have talked about in the book. How can they find out more about you, your website, and your services?

Paul: Well, I welcome everybody to visit my website which is simply www.releasingthepast.com. I have written a lot of content there. If anybody would like to use my therapy services or not, they are going to find something good for themselves there, some perspectives on various kinds of trauma and how to heal it. So, I think there will be value there. People can also, at no charge, download the book you referred to earlier by the name of *Releasing the Past* and look at what those four keys that we were talking about a little while ago are. Of course, if they want to contact me and consider my services and my specialty, which is helping people recover from trauma, then I would certainly welcome that as well.

John: Yeah. I just want to add to that as well, I have to recommend to people to check out your website, and especially watch the video that you have on there and the videos on your YouTube channel because they are very, very well laid out and well thought out. There is great, valuable information that you share there.

Paul: Thank you.

John: That wraps up our interview for today. Paul, I would like to thank you for taking time out of your busy schedule to share your knowledge and expertise. I know people who will listen to this and read this, and they are going to find a lot of value in it, so I would like to thank you on behalf of everyone.

Paul: Well, thank you, John, and thank you to your listeners.

Visit www.JohnMulry.com/book-bonus to download the MP3 audio of this interview.

– 29 –

Bonus Interview with Dax Moy

Who is Dax Moy?

John: Hi guys, it's John Mulry here from the Expect Success Academy and I would like to welcome you to this very special call. This call is another one of the exclusive interviews from my upcoming book, *Your Elephant's Under Threat*. As I have mentioned in the previous one, when I was researching for the book I wanted to seek out the best resources and experts.

One of those experts I have with me today. His name is Dax Moy. Dax is highly regarded not only in the fitness industry but in every industry because at the end of the day, Dax is more than just a coach; he is an inspirer and he is someone who helps you win. Dax is one of the most expensive personal trainers in the world and some of his programs will cost you 20,000 Euro for just a week.

You know, he is highly regarded in the fitness industry because of that and he is a fantastic coach. On top of that, he is also a brilliant trainer and a brilliant leader. He is a fantastic person. When you come in contact with him, his teachings are, "mad ramblings," as he calls them. You cannot help but be inspired. I remember the first time I met Dax was at the FEB in 2012, which was a fitness entrepreneur seminar hosted by John Le Tocq.

From the moment I heard him speak, I resonated with what he was teaching immediately. He went a lot deeper than what most coaches or trainers were willing to go. He challenges us to start holding ourselves to a higher regard. While others are talking tactics and American systems, which I do love by the way, Dax kind of brought it to a whole new level and a step further.

As he discussed, the core desired feelings behind his systems is how, without tapping into these feelings, all the systems and strategies we have and can use are pretty much redundant. A lot of principles and frameworks that he was demonstrating are described in my book, especially the ones related to threat. I have learned these directly from Dax himself. So, I am thrilled to have him on the call and contributing to the book. So thanks, Dax. Thanks again for taking time out of your busy schedule. I really appreciate it.

Dax: No worries, John. What a lovely introduction! Thank you very much. You made me sound like I am pretty cool.

John: You are pretty cool. Trust me.

Dax: Thank you.

Threat Matrix Methodology

John: So, I have some really good questions for you, so we'll get straight into them. The first question is, how did you first learn about and create the Threat Matrix methodology that you teach through your MindMap Course?

Dax: Wow. How long have we got to speak about that? Basically, everything that went into creating the MindMap program really came about through this idea. For far too long, we have considered our clients as being broken, as being weak, as being weak-willed, using things like self-sabotage. As coaches, we thought that way for a very long time. As much as we are meant to improve performance, gym trainers have these labels they like to apply to their clients, their students, their athletes, or whatever. It struck me that this was the easy way out.

That was the side of things that made it sound like there was someone to blame. I wanted to look for things that had nothing to do with blaming but actual pinpointable reasons instead of just saying, "He's been bad," or, "She made a bad choice." We all know that there are better choices than others. We have been given lot of choices on what we can eat, what we can do, how we can move, how we can train. If we know all this stuff, why are we not able to use it?

So it took me into a lot more brain science than most coaches are used to examining. Within that brain science, I was given the first clue, which is essentially that there's a big difference between what most people are trying to accomplish. This is based upon the concept of responses, like planning things and being response-*able* – responsible. And then there are those people that seem to get caught up in reactions over time, with very reactive thinking, reactive actions. There was a huge gap. The huge gap actually turned out to be the difference between a brain-based reflex and a brain-based response.

These things live in different parts of the brain. They are not both on at the same time. Whenever you are in threat, whenever your brain perceives something that it really can't deal with from a threat response setting, so to speak, it will immediately switch to its threat settings. Then you will flicker over into the reactions and so on and so forth. That's the shorter version of how I got there. But it was essentially by asking myself the question, "Where are all the clients that I was working with? Were they all really so weak-willed and weak-minded?" It turns out that, no, that wasn't the answer. The answer is much more than just a simple brain function – that every single one of us has a protection mechanism.

What is threat?

John: Okay so, my next question that you kind of touched on briefly is talking about threat itself. If you were to define threat, how would you put it?

Dax: Well, to define threat, you kind of need to know what safety is first. Because threat lives in the oldest part of the brain, what we call the reptilian mind, but it's not a natural place to be. If we don't spot threat, then the threat trigger should not set off. Okay? So it's easier to come here from the perspective of saying what safety is. Safety is the ability to predict the immediate future and the ability to create the appropriate responses for the immediate environment. That is what safety is. Flip that on its head now and threat is the exact opposite. Threat means anything that affects our ability to predict the immediate future and anything that affects our ability to create an appropriate response to our current environment. That's how we are looking at threat.

That's how we are looking at the overall concept of threat. Because of that, it makes dealing with threat so much easier because what you've got to do is whenever a person is in threat, understand that something about their immediate future, something about their immediate environment is unclear to them, and if you can help them gain clarity by either slowing something down or speeding something up or just helping them get a handle of what the thing is, then their threat will go down and they can go back to being responsible as opposed to reactive.

Ability to Change

John: Okay, so now I'm kind of laser-targeting a little more about what you just said about overcoming that threat. What are your thoughts that our ability to change is limited to how well we can overcome that threat?

Dax: Well, it is exactly that. You will continue to run your threat patterns for as long as threat exists. Your threat patterns are purely reactionary. Reactionary ways of eating, communicating, living, caring for your body, all those things will continue to run. It's a pattern that must run because threat is a survival reflex. So you will continue to run those patterns until the threat is addressed. All change within itself is a threat.

But all change that we desire really begins with moderating that threat. That really comes down to looking at the things in our lives that we are currently afraid of and trying to figure out where a good place to start is. One of the terminologies that we have all heard for years is that *you should face your fear*. The reason why most people won't do it is because the underlying message behind facing your fears has always been to fight your fears, essentially. If you are scared of heights then go somewhere high. If you are scared of the water then get on the water, right? That's how people deem facing your fear to be played out in real life. In reality, facing your fear means literally turning your face toward your fear and looking at it.

"I'm scared of heights. I wonder why I am scared of heights?" and try to figure that out.

Be honest with yourself. Be truthful.

"I'm scared of water. I wonder why I am scared of water."

And try to figure it out as opposed to saying you must suddenly immerse yourself in the thing you fear. So where does that fit in for coaches? A coach starts the journey of change with their clients by having them look at the aspects of their life causing them threat. I am using the word threat, but threat is the same as fear, fear is the same as anxiety, anxiety is the same as stress; there are numerous names for it.

If a client says to you, *"I'm stressed,"* then they are actually speaking the language of threat. If someone tells you, *"I'm anxious,"* they are speaking the language of threat. In fact, if someone talks about being angry, they are also speaking the language of threat. It's looking at what's behind the anxiety, looking at what's behind the fear, looking at what's behind the anger. That's kind of easy to do because we essentially change clients' lives through questions. As really great coaches, we are not here to provide the answers, but we are here to provide really great questions that get people facing whatever the threat is, facing their own fears so they can understand them all.

It's like when you're a kid and you think there's a monster in the wardrobe, right? You are convinced that there's a monster in the wardrobe or under your bed, or wherever it was for you as a kid. We all had one of those monsters somewhere. You could lay there in bed and every night you could be terrified and hoping that it did not come out. But eventually, one day, when you felt sick of feeling that way, you finally opened the cabinet or looked under the bed just to make sure there was nothing there.

The more often you looked, the less scary the cupboard or under the bed became to you. That's pretty much what facing your fear is, to *look* at the things that cause you the fear in the first place. Unless we are actually facing true or life-threatening situations like a building about to collapse or an earthquake or a tornado, something that is about to actually risk our lives, most of our threats are just made up. The stories that we are giving to things like *Mom looked at me in a certain way* or *the guy at the front of the audience pulled that strange face in my introduction because he thinks something different about me than everybody else*. Those are just perceptions, but it does not matter to my brain that it's only a perception. My brain will run them as threats. If my brain is going to run threat stories, then I myself am in charge of the threat stories, right?

I can go back in and say *what does that guy looking at me really mean? Why was Mom a bit annoyed with me today?* Whatever it is. What does that conversation actually *really* mean to you? It does not have to mean what we are making it mean. For me, that is the primary work of a truly great coach. It is to help people create the stories that *serve* them. By helping them make those stories, they don't actually live under threat stories anymore.

Coaching Style

John: Brilliant! How does this model of coaching identify threats and help to overcome them? How does this differ from other models of coaching that are out there?

Dax: Well, to be truthful, most coaching looks and sounds kind of something like this:

"Tell me where you want to go, tell me what you are willing to do to get it, and tell me some of the obstacles that are in the way and I will help you motivate yourself so you can climb over them, crawl under them, smash through them, get rid of them."

Essentially, most coaching is not really coaching. Most coaching is actually much more like a bit of a *rah-rah* session, it's a feel-good session. It's like, *"I believe in you,"* which is great. People need a bit of feel-good. People need a bit of *rah-rah*. People need people to have their back and say, *"I believe in you."* We need all those things, but that's not truly coaching.

We know this because it's kind of the same stuff our moms and dads and people who love us have been doing to encourage us for ages. They have been giving us the *rah-rah* sessions, saying, *"I believe in you, go for it!"* They have been doing that already and it has not worked. At some point, our teachers try the same thing. It does not work. Your partner, your wife, girlfriend, husband, whoever right now, have tried that with you as well and it did not work. *Rah-rah* sessions don't work. But coaching does.

There is a big difference between really coaching and just being a person who's there to motivate. A coach is about helping you become inspired, helping you to inspire yourself, and helping you to find the answers inside yourself as opposed to most coaching, which is instruction-based. It says you've got this obstacle, do this thing. Okay, you've got this fear; this is how you face it. Okay, you've got this struggle, here's how you can *not* struggle anymore. Most coaching generally tends to be very much focused on telling you what to do and instructs you on how to get through the thing.

The MindMap process has nothing to do with instructions. The term we use is extraction; we provide you with the questions so that you extract the answers yourself. First that sounds really, really soft and people are like, *"Wow, I just want to go to a trainer or coach and be told exactly what to do and when to do it."* The truth is no, you don't. Because you have read enough books already by this stage in your life that told you exactly what to do and exactly when to do it. You've read enough magazines that told you exactly what to do and exactly when to do it. You have been given enough advice, let's say from a fitness perspective; you have been given advice by PE teachers, by coaches at your gym, by trainers, by God knows how many TV experts, that kind of stuff. You have been told exactly what to do and when to do it, and you chose not to do it.

So why is that? It's because we want freedom. We don't want to be told what we can and can't do and why we can and can't do it. We want to feel that we are in control of our destiny. In fact, "they are taking away my freedom," is a threat within itself, and one of the biggest ones. "Dax now has to become a John Mulry clone. John told me to eat at 8 o'clock. I must eat at 8 o'clock. He told me to eat eggs. I must eat eggs."

Nobody wants that kind of life. We are all seeking freedom. What the MindMap program does is help you create working frameworks for your own life by having *you* create them; they're not being given to you by the coach. From that perspective it's a very, very different place. It's a place where you are not surrounded by judgment. You are not surrounded by a pure concept of right and wrong, the right way to do things, the wrong way to do things. If something doesn't serve you, you are simply asked to figure out how to make it serve you or be okay with it not serving you.

I still like a really nice glass of red wine on weekends. I don't believe red wine's particularly good for me but there's something about it I enjoy. My life would be diminished slightly in the absolute absence, permanently for the rest of my life, of a really nice glass or two of red wine on the weekends. It's a choice that I make without any stories around it (it's good for me, it's got reservatrol, etc.). Actually no, I just really love this, the feeling, the taste, the smell. Those things combined and how it makes me relax. Those things combined actually add to the quality of my life, right?

Define

Sure, this is not just for threat. This is for anything you want as well. It goes equally for what you want and for what you don't want. It starts with define. Define is really simple. A lot of people are chasing a lot of things that they don't have clarity around. They say they want to get into that size 10 jeans or whatever, they are currently size 14 or 16. So, size 10 jeans become their goal. You ask them why their reaching it is so important and they don't really have much of a back story.

Here's the trick. If you really want to have a size 10 pair of jeans and you are size 16, you would have already been in size 10 jeans because you really want it. So, something in you doesn't really want it the way you said you do, and when it comes down to it, you don't really want to have the size 10 jeans. You'd enjoy them as a side effect. But there's something behind that. We call it *peeling the onions*. So we rip that away.

Why do you want the size 10 jeans?
I want the size 10 jeans because it will make me feel more confident.

Why is it important for you to feel confident?

Because it will make me feel more sexy.

Why is it important for you to feel sexy?
Because it will strengthen the bonds between myself and my husband because I feel we've been drifting apart and going separate ways.

Can you see it already? It's like three layers of onion down. You've got a much bigger reason. *"I want to get in great shape because I feel I am losing my husband because of the lack of intimacy and lack of connection."* That is just one example. It is a very common one that I hear from a lot of people. It's not about changing yourself to suit your husband; it's about changing yourself if and only if you really want to because of how it serves you. The size 10 jeans would never create that level of inspiration for most people, right? But holding their marriage together would. And falling back in love with the person they once fell in love with and having them fall back. Now there's a much bigger connection to seeing through the diet and seeing through the exercise changes or anything else that may be going on. So, definition becomes extremely important.

Refine

Dax: Next is refine. You mostly make refinements to your goals by really determining what you don't want. I call it untying the nots. It's just one of the exercises. Untying the nots is about saying what do I *not* want to be in the situation, who do I *not* want to be, what things am I determined *not* to engage in during the course of today, this week, this month, this year in my life, who am I *not* going to be. A lot of us have a lot of trouble identifying the things that we really *do* want. You ask a person, essentially, what do you want to be when you grow up? And they're like, I don't know, I'm not really sure. There are so many choices to be made or so many jobs I could do, so many countries I could live in. It's confusing.

Your Elephant's Under Threat

Choice makes life confusing. But the refinement process makes it a lot easier because it shuts down choices. It now says, you are the same person, you don't know what job you want to do or what country you want to live in. What job would you definitely *not* love to do? That person will come up with a shopping list of jobs that they would hate to do. I don't want to do this. I'd hate to be in an office day long. I don't want to wear a suit. I don't want this. Okay. You just described the whole bunch of jobs that we could have spent months for you to try and see if they're the right fit for you and you just told me exactly what you don't want, so we can shut down those areas in the map. We can also do the same thing as far as your partner.

You ask someone exactly what they want in a partner and they've got these very vague pictures of what he or she should look like, how he or she might dress. You ask them what they *don't* want in a partner and their shopping list is huge. I don't want him to speak to me like this, I don't want him to treat me like that, I don't want this other thing.

That is the refinement process of really digging down and identifying where the nots are. There are other elements to it but that's the core of where it starts.

Align

Dax: Then the alignment process. Define, refine, align. The alignment process is really quite simple. It's about asking yourself before you ever step foot on a journey, before you take the very first step, what would be the most enjoyable first step that you could take? When I say enjoyable, I say it wouldn't create too much fear or threat for you. It would excite you.

So it's a big step to get you moving but it's a small enough step to have you believe that you can do it. What would the next step be and the next step after that? How are you going to make sure that every step of the journey is something you find enjoyable? It does not mean that there are no hard parts to it. It does not mean there are no struggles. But you can still enjoy a struggle, you can still enjoy hard work, right?

But what you can't enjoy are things that make you feel disconnected from yourself, things that make you feel like you have to give up all the best things in life, all the things that you love in order to get something that you are not even certain that you will get. The alignment process is all about designing a journey that is going to be one that you say to yourself, "Wow, I could really see myself doing this and enjoying this and loving every step of it." In my mind, it's not worth starting a journey if you are already dreading it, which is again where most people think, *"Oh god, I'm starting this diet on Monday. Thank God it's only 30 days."*

They are already looking forward to it being over. That is a journey not worth taking: a journey that you cannot wait to get behind you. *"God, I can't believe I have to do this."* That's a journey probably not worth taking. The alignment is about kind of identifying a journey that you are going to be absolutely madly, passionately in love with because it makes you look and feel and perform. You feel great doing it.

In a nutshell, that's define, refine, and align. Again, I understand it sounds so soft because we have been used to our trainers or coaches cracking a whip over us and saying, "For every success there's a price to pay." It's true, for every success there is a price to pay. But we have control over how fast we are going to pay that. Most people cannot pay their mortgage in one hit. If somebody said, "Okay, you just bought this house a week ago, so pay $250 grand today." Most people would never be able to have the house, would they? *"Crap, I don't have $250 grand in the bank."* That's the truth for most people. But how do we get to pay on that house so that one day we own it? For a very long, protracted period of time, we pay much smaller amounts so we eventually own the house, right? We get to control the journey ourselves. Just like most of us who get to choose how we pay our mortgage, we get to choose how long you want to pay the price to any goal, any accomplishment, any feeling, any experience.

You get to choose how long you are going to take to do it. You could completely transform your body in 30 days, absolutely. I have helped people to do that. But very few people transform and keep that 30-day transformation because the journey was so terrible. What will make the journey just like most of us choose how to pay the mortgage? What will make the journey as enjoyable as possible is the alignment question.

Top Three Questions

John: Brilliant! So then, you just talked briefly about how you help your coaching clients. From your own coaching clients that you have, what are the top three questions that you get from them and how do you answer them?

Dax: Top three questions, right? I guess that in many respects, there are the same questions from everyone. It's just that they were asked through different words. The core question behind everything is really, *"How can I be happy?"* Every goal pursuit, like that size 10 jeans or losing 30lbs, how can I better communicate with my boyfriend or my husband, they have all got something to do with happiness.

So, at the core of everything really, a lot of my clients are asking me how they can be happy. I am very clear about that from the outset. I just spoke about peeling the onion, right? We all have different things in each layer of the skin on that onion. But what lies in the core of that onion for every single one of us I believe is happiness; we are all trying to get to be happy. If you know that from the outset as a coach, you know that final destination on the map is happy, but how people define happy is different, then all of your questions from that point forward can all just be about, "Will this make you happy? Is this a way to make you happy?"

You can change these words because they may not express the exact word *happy* to me, but they might say, "What is the fastest way to lose 30 pounds? What is the easiest way to lose 30 pounds?" One of the things as a coach in terms of building the map is that I remember that the client is always in charge of the journey. In terms of building this map, I want to help them design the best possible pace.

The best possible pace comes down to this: do you want the fastest possible journey which is, to be honest, going to be probably the harshest? It's going to be one where you have to make the biggest changes, make the most demands, and kind of suffer a little bit more if you want to put it that way. Are they really looking for the fastest possible way? If so, I would be telling them what fast actually entails. We can do fast. But you are not going to eat the foods that you like. You are not going to do these things. You have to do this and this and this. Most people think that they want the fastest possible route to get somewhere when really what they want is something different. So then, I offer them the easiest option. The easy way sounds beautiful.

The easiest way to lose 30 pounds, you could say, is easy because it's a very slow and protracted journey, where you make very, very few changes at all. Maybe you are just committed to losing a pound a week for the next 30 weeks, or even half a pound a week, or just nibble away it. The trouble with the easiest journey is that it often does not bring back the kind of results they are looking for in a timeframe they feel good about. It feels like they are not getting anywhere.

Dax: The easiest journey is often the one that causes the most frustration for people because everything feels too slow. If you remember from the program, the real threat is about speed, something happening too fast or something happening too slowly. We've almost got this Goldilocks principle: that was too hot, that was too cold. Well, what is just right?

The third option is, are you interested in the fastest, the slowest, or the best route to get to where you want to go? The best is not a route defined by me: it's a route defined by them. When I am working with people, explaining to them the concept of keeping their results because they feel comfortable keeping on with the journey is always a part of what the best way includes. You probably don't want to continue the journey if it's just so slow and you get bored of it. If it's something too fast, you may actually get to your destination but you can't wait to stop.

But the best possible journey is the one that you love, the one that you enjoy, the one that you are going to keep on with even once you reach the destination. You'll get there and think, "Okay, I've lost the 30 pounds but I still want to continue with that because this diet makes me feel great. This exercise makes me feel brilliant." That would be where I go with that. In terms of three questions, the questions are a combination of essentially how can I be happy and a mix of the fastest, the easiest, and the best. Hopefully that makes sense.

Advice to People Who are Feeling Stuck

John: Perfect! It really illustrates perfectly something I try to get across in the book as well so that's great. Just for someone who is feeling stuck, who can't move forward in their life whether it's intermittent health, a relationship, or in their business, but then they don't quite understand the power of coaching or they don't quite value the power of coaching, what would you say to that person who is feeling stuck?

Dax: What I would say is that, when you are in the midst of threat, you can't see your own solutions. It's because of the way the brain has been designed. When you are in threat, you are in the reactive part of the brain, which is what we call the reptilian brain at its lowest level. You are in that part. And the reptilian brain does not think, it reacts. So you become extremely reactive. Reactive means that you play over the same old programs again and again. What we need is to help you get to the responsive part of the brain; the responsive part of the brain is the frontal cortex.

You can't access that while you are under threat. You can't ask the right questions. You can't do so many of the things that you need to do in order to get you unstuck. But a coach can. At this level we're talking about a professional coach, but a coach can be anybody who is outside of your game. They are not usually your wife, your husband, your partner, your girlfriend, your mom, your dad. They are not usually the people who love you. They can be at times, but they are not usually the people who love you. They are normally the people who are detached from your game who are not going to give you any form of biased information just because they love you or don't want to hurt your feelings. They're not going to try and steer you based upon what *they* think is right.

Your parents and your family, and everybody else, they all do it with a very well-meaning heart, I'm certain, but they're always going to have part of their own best interest at heart as they give you the answer. That's the nature of family, of love coaching. A real coach is basically going to stay outside and hold up the mirror to you in terms of showing you how you've been answering these questions. Instead of saying, yes, that's right, that's wrong, they are going to ask you questions in the right way which is going to lead to you coming out with your *own* definitions and taking your *own* journey.

The real danger of any other form of coaching, pseudo-coaching or family coaching, is that you are always being influenced to kind of take somebody else's journey. Let's do something kind of difficult. Let's say you are coaching with your wife or your husband. Actually as they hear you talk, the things that come out in their mind is that you are really unhappy with the relationship and the best possible thing for you would be to end it. Your husband or wife are very unlikely to say to you, "Sitting here listening you talk I think the best possible thing for you to do would be to end this relationship." Because they are *in* the game. But look, here's the flipside of this, a truly great coach would not be saying that, either. They would not be saying that out of avoidance, they would ask you questions about how you feel about your relationship so you actually gain better clarity.

Maybe what comes out at the end of it is that you realize you have a relationship worth fighting for and that you would rather stay with it but you know you've got some work to do. A truly great coach, I have seen some truly amazing coaches out there over the time that I have been running around my programs and educating people through them, a truly great coach can have you ask yourself the questions, have you taking the action that really matters to help you get to the place that will make you most happy in life. That is the definition of a coach. Someone who helps you find your happiness.

John: The analogy I use for that is to imagine a player/manager vs. a complete manager. The player/manager is in the game the whole time so he cannot look from a 30,000-foot view of the actual game and see what's fully going on, whereas if you have a dedicated coach on the outside looking in, he could see a lot more of what's going on. He can help you make better decisions yourself from that aspect because he's got a different perspective. If you are in the game the whole time you kind of get sucked into that environment as well and you can't see a way out.

Find Out More About Dax Moy and His Programs

John: Okay Dax, that was brilliant. One final question just about yourself: if anyone who has been listening or to anyone who reads this, how can they find out more about you and your programs that you offer, just to follow you along or to hear your stories or your articles that you wrote? How can they find out more about you?

Dax: Sure. I am in a bunch of places. My new website is daxfitlife.com, where basically all my programs for the public, my mad ramblings, and my coaching basic log, that all sits there. Then I've got fitsystemtraining.com where I educate personal trainers in terms of the three maps coaching process. We have spoken about the MindMap, there's also the BodyMap and the BioMap, different elements of mapping out who we are and how we do the things we do. That's where you can find me. You can also find me on Facebook. Literally, just facebook.com/daxmoy.

John: Perfect. Okay Dax, I just want to thank you again for taking the time out of your busy schedule. I hope you enjoy the rest of your time in Florida.

Dax: No worries, man. I really enjoyed it. Thanks for having me as a guest.

Visit www.JohnMulry.com/book-bonus to download the MP3 audio of this interview.

– 30 –

Bonus Interview with Brian Grasso

Who is Brian Grasso?

Brian has enjoyed a diverse and successful life, from being the CEO of the largest and most internationally-acclaimed organization within the fitness and sports industry worldwide to being featured in different media centres from the New York Times to Men's Health.

A former performance coach, Brian has trained more than 20,000 athletes worldwide including Olympic Gold Medalists, World Champions, and professionals from various sports (NHL, CFL, NFL, and MLB). He retired at the young age of 37 from the fitness industry and founded FTR Nation, or Freethinking Renegade. I first came across Brian in May of last year, when he completely uplifted, empowered, and inspired me and many others at Birmingham University.

One thing that struck me the most about Brian is that he's good at bringing words together in such a way that does not just motivate you but ignites that inner spark, that inner fire that compels you to look deep inside and question the path that you are on. Since first meeting Brian, I can honestly say that he's completely changed the way I see my life unfolding. Through his incredible movie "Life by Numbers" and the book *Audacity of Success*, I have begun a journey that is unique to me because he inspired me to ignore the rules and follow my true path in life. Brian, I am truly honored to have you with me and I am excited for everyone who will be listening to or reading this.

Brian: Oh, thanks for all that, brother. I certainly appreciate it, man. I hope the information you get lives up to all that.

John: Yeah, I am sure it will. We will get straight into some of the questions. As you know, the main premise today is talking about uncovering your reason why and that it is really, really powerful in aligning everything to move forward.

I believe you just make a big, big difference. And your own life story is very powerful and more than deserves to be spread far and wide because it's so inspiring. Can you re-tell the story for everyone here?

Brian's Fitness Career

Brian: My 'whys' are actually multi-dimensional, and one of the greatest 'why' stories that I have I want to set up in advance a little bit. I was like this in my past as well and I think it is very, very common in our world that people spend a lot more time asking themselves, "how?" We have dreams. We have goals. We have ambitions. We have intentions. There are largely two prohibiting factors that I have seen in my world, in my life, and in working with so many people worldwide that prevent us from going after those changes.

Subconscious Programming

The first of these is subconscious programming. I think we live in such a goal-setting nirvana world wherein we are all taught to set and achieve goals, and there are a number of works that talk about goals and how you achieve them, etc.

But I am really not fond of the whole propagation that you cannot out-goal-set an unsuccessful mindset. The subconscious programming we have is so powerful but it is so hidden we don't necessarily know it's there. It is based on factors that transcend our entire life: the parents we have, the way that we are spoken to as children; our relationships with people, affection, food, fitness, intellectual stimulation, and creativity... so much of who we are is based on the conditioning patterns of our culture, our country, our immediate family, our parents, and because of that we adopt what I call *absolute truths*.

Truth

We see the world in a certain way from our eyes. There is a great danger in that. For example you, John, and I, are standing in the same room, and we are looking at a chair. You are standing at the one side of the chair. I am standing at the other side of the chair. There are reasons intrinsic to you and intrinsic to me that cause you and me to see the chair in very different ways.

Partially because of our eyes. You have your eyes your entire life and I have my eyes my entire life, so the things we notice are going to be very different just based on our conditioning patterns of how we look at the chair. Those are the intrinsic things. There are also extrinsic things. When the sun shines in the window, it is illuminating or refracting light off of a certain part of the chair that is more on your side than mine. You see that refraction, I might not. It might not be notable to me as much it is to you. I say that there are no absolute truths.

There is nothing in life that is absolutely true for you and for me at the same time except death. One day you are going to die. One day I am going to die. That is an absolute truth. But how we see the world, how we perceive the world is not absolutely true.

It is just a product of the conditioning that we have incurred in the story we process. I say that as one really key factor for why versus how. In that whole monitor of our eyes, whenever we ask how, we are only forming answers that are based on our current level of understanding, what our eyes have seen in the world. If we have someone who is 40 years old and an executive, they make stable money, they are not particularly fulfilled in life but they are safe. Yet inside their heart they want to go on to build a company or travel the world.

If they are going to ask themselves, "how do I do that?" It's their conditioning influence that they would be drawing the answers from. Their conditioning influence might say, "I can't do that because I have a stable career, I must stay in this stable career." So we run into dangers and we ask how, which is why I learned a long time ago to ask myself why. It's not going to matter how I am going to do it; it is why I want to.

Sawubona!

The most influential story for me as it relates to my why actually occurred in 2006 or 2007. I was in Melbourne, Australia. I was asked to lecture on the concepts of Youth Athlete Development. Most always the case, the organisers end up taking the presenters out for dinner during the course of the conference at some point. I found myself on an outdoor patio enjoying salmon and spinach, which was the meal I was having while engrossed in conversation with a man named Douglas who was from South Africa.

He was also one of the presenters there at this conference. He and I were talking about language and how language has become a very informal communication pattern in our world. Text, Facebook, private messages, Twitter; it's almost like we abbreviate everything. We don't express ourselves.

Whenever anyone writes with a particular flair, it's almost too thick for people, people will not understand it. But these are English words! I mean they are words easy to understand. Douglas and I were talking about that. We started talking about the way we greet people and how it is so standard to say, "Hey, how are you doing?" "What's up?" or, "What's going on?"

Those are questions, yet we ask them routinely and almost always do not care what the answer is. We are not even expecting an answer. That got me thinking a great deal about what I really understood in this conversation, and as it turns out, Douglas introduced me to a word. The word is *sawubona*. It is a Zulu word that is used by his natives in South Africa as a greeting. *Sawubona* translates to English as, "I see you." I had such veneration for this word, this concept of the word, as Douglas was telling me the story. For all intents and purposes, it means that when we pass each other in the street we actually stop, we don't just wing by each other. We stop.

We say *sawubona,* meaning, "I see you; I am paying attention to you; I am actually taking you in; I am sharing this moment with you," not thinking about being late to that appointment or, "I don't know this guy that well so I am not going to waste my time standing here talking."

They spend time in moments with each other, sharing the moment of communication. They see each other. That is so beautiful. But the true crux of my why was based on when I was flying back home from Melbourne. I was on the plane back to Chicago, where I lived at that time, and I was just mulling over the whole concept of *sawubona* in my head and I started thinking about everything in our world and how it seems so glorious to externalize things.

We are charitable outwardly. We love outwardly, we are compassionate outwardly. *Sawubona,* I see you, something we draw outward to other people. It hit me like a lightning bolt, how all of that needs to be brought inside.

In order to love truly we have to love ourselves and feel compassion to other people, we have to be compassionate for our own infallibilities. In order to be charitable, truly altruistic, we have to apply that same spirit to ourselves. In order to see other people, we have to see ourselves. It is a great mirage that we live and die in, never having truly grasped or understood or even wanted to.

Conditioning Pattern

But we live in a world of projecting outward. And I often say in this job that, if your best friend talks to you the way you talk to yourself in your head, you would never talk to your friend again, you would hate them. Yet look at the way we talk to ourselves. We don't love ourselves; we get angry at ourselves. We get spiteful towards ourselves. We get mad at the decisions we make or don't make. We get belligerent towards ourselves.

We are so busy pushing love out and pushing compassion out, pushing benevolence and altruism out. We need to bring it inside. Before we see people, we need to see ourselves. What do I really want? This is my life. This is my life. This is my life. This is not about paying my bills. I often say, "How many people quantify work as a necessary evil?" Your working life, overturn of your life, constitutes about 63%-65%. So, we are willing to trade more than half our life and qualify it as a necessary evil just to pay the bills.

I do not believe that is reasonable. I believe that is why Henry David Thoreau wrote things like, "most men die with songs of passion still in their hearts." That was my big 'why' moment in my life where I realized that I cannot just know that I have dreams in my heart; I have to know what they are and I have to pursue them. The reason why I am pursuing them is because that is what life is supposed to be.

Life has become complex because our perspective is that it is complex. Our conditioning patterns have taught us to believe that it is complex. But there is a great simplicity in knowing why you have a dream and why it is imperative to pursue it. Not how, just why. That is my why's greatest moment. It changed my world.

John: Thank you. That's fantastic how you talk about that because a lot of people, myself included, fell into that trap. A lot of people tend to focus on the 'how' and the 'what' and neglect the 'why.'

How versus Why

Brian: I think one of the reasons goes back to conditioning. If you were to peruse any bookstore in the world, the largest section is self-help, which I actually think is moronic. Because self-help, the very word "self-help," if you look at it, the implication is self-help: "I am broken. I need to fix something." Self-help = I am broken. That is what self-help implies.

I do not think that self-help is the right context. I think what we should be looking at is self-actualization, becoming our truest self. I am not broken. You are not broken. I do not surmise that anyone is broken. What I believe to be true is that we have deep understandings and awareness inside of us and we know we have to understand them. That does not make us broken.

That makes us beautiful, spiritual creatures in need of drawing awareness to it. I think one of the reasons people ask how more than why is because, in that nirvana of self-help, 1/3 to 2/3 of the books you are going to find are about goals.

Goal Development

Goal development or goal setting is always about, "what do I want and how am I going to get it?" That is what we have been conditioned to believe is the most appropriate way of obtaining what we want. But if you think about it, and what I'm suggesting, is to look at why in the context of *sawubona*: what do you *actually* want? Because I think it is deeper. I think that, one, we look at how because we are so taught via conditioning of goal setting to ask, "What do you want and *how* do you want to achieve it?"

That is one. But in the absence of truly going inside the job, do we even know what we really want? Is that not part of the

problem? Very often, our goals are manufactured products of what we see the rest of the world wanting in terms of goals. We automatically attune goals with money. Goals mean houses and cars. Goals mean spouses and businesses. Because that is the standard response, and standard response is in our conditioning. If that is what most of society that influences us deems worthy, then our conditioning setup is that we deem it worthy.
But people romanticise the idea of the truth that you can't take money with you, that I would rather be happy, fulfilled, and rich, yet when we talk about happy and fulfilled, we talk about money. So I think that there are multiple reasons why people investigate how more than why. I think one of them is conditioning that we are used to.

I think people who are reading this right now might not even realise that asking themselves why is something that they know they should do. It is not conditioning. What I also think is that a deeper level indicates that we are not truly going inside ourselves to discover the what. It is actually *what* do we want. It is a superficial want based on conditioning to the first question we ask, which is *how* we are going to do it.

When you get to the stuff you *really* want to do, those incredibly deep passions that are in your heart, it's almost like we don't need a blueprint. We just need permission to do it. All of a sudden we do it without a blueprint, without any 'how.' Does that make sense?

Living Life with Audacity

John: It really, really does. One other passion of yours is to live life with audacity. So can you explain this and the freedom that it provides?

Brian: Yeah, audacity. It is one of those words in the English language that people adore because it has a dualistic meaning. Contemporarily, most people will look at the word audacity as negative. "To have the audacity to do something like that," implies the way we use it colloquially now. It implies that we have done something wrong. There is a negative about it.

But the word actually means bold. It means daring. That's what audacity means from a definition perspective. There's a dualistic meaning of it where we seem to adopt it or gravitate towards the negative version. There's a positive part in audacity which is bold and daring.

Free Thinking Renegades

The reason Free Thinking Renegades is called Free Thinking Renegades is not at all because I am hoping to inspire people to confound societal expectations as a matter of negativity. Meaning I am not hoping to inspire people to be rebels for no reason. If conformity says, "Do that just because," that is not my intention. My intention is to inspire people to be truly free thinking. In that respect, look at societal norms. Look at conformist tendencies. Look at context and perspective. Most people walk into society and simply become whatever the cogs in the wheel are supposed to become. It's absent thinking if these rules and regulations are things that they happen to agree with. The free thinking component is not about effacing societal standards. It is simply considering whether or not those standards should apply to you.

Brian: The renegade portion of the company, the renegade work is simply if they don't apply to you, be a renegade and do your own thing, on your terms, in the way that you decide is best for yourself. I would surmise that a lot of people in society are broken, broke, sad, unfulfilled, and unhappy. I think most people will agree with that if they look around.

That being our case, why do those people get to dictate to us what right or wrong is? They shouldn't. We all get to have free will. Free will means we have got to do our own thinking, our own bidding. Audacity is the freedom to question if societal conformist tendencies and societal norms are going to apply to me the way they apply to everybody else.

Audacity via renegadism is simply to say that, if I decide that societal norms don't apply to what I want, then I will be audacious and I have to take action in ways that I feel are best. Audacity is the most freeing concept in the world to believe every single day of your life. You don't have to do it the way it's commonly done. Do it your way. That, by the way, scares the living crap out of people, because we seek shelter and stability in conformity. When we realise we do, it is so freeing. It is a path that sometimes we have to march slowly towards because it can be scary for a lot of people.

John: Exactly. I think that you are right about what audacity brings and the freedom that it provides. The ultimate thing that you strive towards is to have that personal freedom. To know that the choices you make are your own and you will go down the path that is unique to you. You are choosing to go down that path because it is the right one for you.

When I first saw your short movie, "Life by Numbers," it immediately struck me and struck the cards. I initially questioned my own path: *"Was that actually my own?"* I realised that, at that time, it was not. I was not going down a path that I thought I should have been going down. It is similar when I read your book, *Audacity of Success*. The two together, the movie and the book, are not just a marriage of words. It is where words make you. You don't have to bring words together in order. They are much more than that. It is something that is trying to internally question you: *"Why do you do what you do?"* On your book and movie, why did you decide to put it all on the table for everyone to see? How do you grow as a person doing that?

Life by Numbers and Audacity of Success

Brian: Oh, brilliant. Yes. Thank you. That's a really good question. I never get asked that question. I have always wanted to get asked that question because it is one I think about all the time. The human condition comes with several things, one of which is that we are not infallible. I have ego just like everybody else in the world has ego.

I teach the concept of being aware of one's ego, finding where you can see the healthy ego vs. the unhealthy ego and how to react accordingly based on awareness. That really helps me sharpen my own perception, my own understanding of my own ego, when I might be sitting in it unhealthily and acting in a way that is disproportionate to how I actually feel. Life by Numbers and Audacity of Success serve me in exactly the same way.

Life by Numbers

Life by Numbers, ironically, I wrote in just a matter of an hour, very late one night after caring for my fiancée when she was ill with the flu and had gone to bed early. I decided to write because I love to write in the evening hours. I find the moon and all that very romantic and inspirational, so I just sat there and wrote chronically these thoughts that I'd been having for years about conformity and if we regret at our end of days, the day we die, regret will be paralysing for some people if we do not sharpen our wits in terms of realising and recollecting what we have done, what we are doing, and why we are doing it.

That came out of me in an hour. There's very few days that go by that I do not reflect on words in that movie. Where I remember writing lines like, "Buying a living room set that matches because we are afraid to not fit in." We have just always gone the way of the path rather than forging our own trail. Those are the things that are like monsters in my life. It's an ethos that I am reminded of daily because, like everybody else, I have distractions.

What I mean by that is I have bills to pay; I have two kids; should I have a more stable career or whatever? It is in the best interest for my own kids. I have thoughts like that just like everybody else. Life by Numbers really helped me, and still to this day it does. It has helped form my ethos, the way I sort of remind myself of the things that are important to me.

Audacity of Success

Audacity of Success was not different. It was just a longer way of saying it all to be honest, but I draw great strengths from that book, multiple times in a week. I think my favorite thing in terms of that book and reflecting about it, it's obviously seven chapters, and the seven parts of my own creed, my own credo and ethos for living. What I have noticed happens is that, day to day when I see evidence of myself following a kind of path or being audacious or being authentic, I think I become very happy with the fact that the ethos is clearly so alive in me. That writing all that stuff has given me pause to realise how much I live it and how much I am thirsty to live it more every single day.

More on Brian Grasso

John: That is amazing. The book and the movie I recommend to everyone because it makes you question things. You question your path. Just on that, how can people find out more about you and your incredible book and movie?

Brian: I appreciate that. Well, the best place to find me is freethinkingrenegades.com. That is our blog. That is just countless amounts of freedom information there. We have been posting blogs and courses for a long time there. It's all just there. It's all free. You can find *Audacity of Success* and Life by Numbers via links on that one website. My strongest suggestion is to go to freethinkingrenegades.com.

John: Very good, Brian. I would like to thank you once again for taking time out of your busy schedule. I really appreciate that. You have shared a lot today. I have learned a lot just interacting with you. I am going to continue to learn from you because you have a lot to give and I would like to thank you for that. Thank you so much.

Brian: My honor. Thank you so much for inviting me, John. It was my privilege.

Visit www.JohnMulry.com/book-bonus to download the MP3 audio of this interview.

John Mulry, MSc

– 31 –

The Missing Chapter

"Effort only fully releases its reward after a person refuses to quit."

– Napoleon Hill

I think I'm a lot like you. I take my business really seriously.

At the end of the day, the reason we as entrepreneurs run our business and don't work for someone else is because we want to have control over our financial futures. We want to be able to determine how much we can earn and we want our businesses to make us money. A strong mission for your business is wise, but unless your business is earning you profit, it's not a business.

That was one of the main reasons I started my own business in the first place, so I could be in control of and not be controlled. The whole idea of someone telling me I was only worth a certain salary didn't sit well with me at all. I'm sure you're the same. How dare someone try and tell us what we're worth, right?

For these reasons, I take my business seriously as I'm sure you do, too. At the same time, I want my business to provide me with the energy, time, freedom, and income to live the life that I want. Spend time with the people I love. To be able to take trips away to places like New York, London, or wherever I please and not worry about whether my business will be there when I get back.

The problem there is that business is changing. As an entrepreneur or a small business owner, the pressure we're under can be enormous. Too often the odds are stacked against us small business owners.

The stats on businesses having to close since 2008 are shocking. Over 48,000 small businesses in Ireland closed due to the recession. The added pressure this number puts on existing businesses is arguably just as bad.

This is especially true when it comes to the most important part of your business: marketing, advertising, and sales. When I first started my business I had no money for traditional media advertising. I had a little savings but wasn't confident enough in advertising in newspapers or radio and honestly I didn't know anything about them.

I wasn't sure any campaigns I'd run would be successful. Success is important to me.

I wasn't looking for a million euro marketing campaign. I wanted a successful, reliable, low-risk, and unique approach to acquiring and nurturing clients and prospects. I wanted a way to acquire the clients I love working with, not ones I dread.

I wasn't about to gamble my money away and end up back in the corporate finance world I hated, the one I left behind.

I'll tell you something else, I didn't like the idea of handing my money over to some agency on some ad or some campaign that may or may not work. I wanted something proven, as I'm sure you do, a system for getting and keeping all the clients I could handle.

Have you ever been approached or 'cold called' into buying advertising space, spending your marketing budget on ads in newspapers and online without ever fully understanding what you were spending your money on? And have you managed to track and consistently measure your ROI (return on investment) on that advertising?

Luckily for me, I discovered somebody who has been helping owners of businesses and salespeople in over 200 types of businesses increase their income, dramatically and fast….solve all their advertising and prospecting problems….and make their business lives better. He's world famous so I'm embarrassed to say I'd never heard of him before. Maybe you have, maybe you haven't. But in a very short time, he made such a huge, positive impact in my business, and life that, given the opportunity to partner with him and coordinate a local group of business owners in a unique kind of 'mastermind group,' to work together applying his strategies and help each other, I jumped at it.

This is where it starts to get interesting.

For all entrepreneurs and small business owners who would like to continue reading "The Missing Chapter," please visit:

www.JohnMulry.com/missing-chapter

John Mulry, MSc

– 32 –

Frequently Asked Questions

for

John and the Expect Success Academy

What is the Expect Success Academy?

With the Expect Success Academy, I consult with and provide small business owners and entrepreneurial professionals with the systems, strategies, and tools they need to get more clients, build strong relationships, handle change with ease, and unlock the untapped potential in their businesses faster than they could ever do on their own.

What is Business 2.0 Strategy?

Business 2.0 Strategy encompasses what I call the new rules for local businesses. It is made up of seven key pillars:

- Client experience
- Direct response marketing
- Expectancy of success
- Focus on fundamentals
- Pre-emptive value adding
- Relationship building
- Systems and strategy

Can You Help My Business?

That depends; are you willing to have an open mind and take on broad new ideas and strategies that will enable you to work less, earn more, and nurture your prospects into long-term repeat clients? If yes, then I can certainly help you.

What About Your Private Membership Group?

I have finalised a partnership with serial entrepreneur and 'Millionaire Maker' Dan Kennedy and GKIC to launch Ireland's first GKIC private monthly membership group. This group encompasses coaching, networking, accountability, soundboarding, business building systems, and strategies as well as providing small business owners, entrepreneurs, and sales professionals with the opportunity to work *on* their business instead of *in* their business.

For more info and to join this group, visit:

www.JohnMulry.com/GKIC

Do You Offer Coaching?

I do offer coaching but it isn't for everybody. You have to want explosive growth and you need to be honest enough to answer some testing questions, which if answered openly, could transform your business and life overnight. You'll be amazed at what you can do with your sudden, newfound ability to deal with everything that comes your way.

I'm not looking to pressure you into requesting more information or applying. In fact, I've decided to be pretty picky about whom I work with. You have to apply and not all applications will be accepted. You also have to agree to my four "Expect Success Principles" before applying. I want to ensure the people I work with are committed to getting results.

What are Your Four Expect Success Principles?

1. Expect Success Principle of Expectation

I approach each and every client the same way. First I let you know what you can expect from me and then let you know what I expect from you. I will devote myself to you and your business just as I would with any other client. We will demystify how to grow your business. There are only three basic ways and one advanced way. Next I will give you the simple knowledge, skills, and strategies you need so your business is set up to give you exactly what you want.

2. Expect Success Principle of Family

My family and private life are more important than you and I expect that you would agree that your family is more important than me. There may be times where we must choose between work and family, and we should choose family.

3. Expect Success Principle of Mutual Respect

I am working with you, not for you, so we must treat each other with respect. I will respect your time and I expect you to respect mine.

4. Expect Success Principle of Value

I am not cheap. My fees are not time-based. They are based on the ultimate value of what I provide for you in terms of systems, strategy, focus, accountability, and outcome as well as my own unique experiences and education. If you are looking for cheap, I will gladly recommend you to someone else who may serve your monetary needs.

Will You Speak at My Event?

Yes, I can speak at your event whether it's a full on seminar or a more intimate private affair. Topics I speak on include but are not limited to:

- Positive thinking versus positive doing
- Your Elephant's Under Threat
- The new rules for local business marketing
- Go with the giving hand
- How to build long lasting relationships with customers and clients
- How to laugh at the "Down Economy"
- 13 advertising mistakes that are crippling your business

- Direct response and online marketing for local businesses
- Work/life balance for the busy professional
- The forgotten art of being a value adder

What about Workshops?

I occasionally run in-depth and actionable workshops on the topics above and other areas ranging from positive change, direct response marketing, and online marketing. If your business, association, or organisation is large enough and would like to know about what workshops are available and how you can benefit from them, you can fill out an expression of interest application.

How Can I Get Started?

To get started, simply visit www.JohnMulry.com

Additional Praise for John and the Expect Success Academy

"John Mulry, you are God damn amazing; I hope this is included in the testimonial. You have changed my attitude, my daily life is now easier and more refreshing since I started with the Expect Success Academy team. You can't put into words how grateful and appreciative I am for all your attention and cooperation. You have put a smile and swagger back in my step, something which is priceless."

–Kevin Nugent, MD, Mr. Waffle, Galway Ireland

"Expect Success Academy has changed my life. I'm more positive as John instills that belief and 'can do' attitude into you. The main thing for me was having trust in someone who is going to be committed to me and my goals. John ensures you meet your goals and stay on the right track. Believe in yourself & John Mulry and you'll get amazing results. Simple."

–Stephen Hardiman, Senior Manager, Dunnes Stores, Galway, Ireland

"John, great presentation last night. Loved it, very informative, exciting, and engaging. The humour and metaphors, it stands out and I will remember it. Get him to speak, very motivational and very smart."

–Maricka Burke Keogh, Online Marketing in Galway, Galway, Ireland

"I just wanted to say that I thought the material you presented this evening was really fresh and interesting and really relevant! I really admire your branding and new ideas. You have a great mind! What I took from the evening is don't take people for granted, especially clients who are 'under my protection.' In that sense, really look after them with care, build a relationship in every way possible and appreciate the value of this, and understand that the 'sell my shit' stuff don't work anymore and a lot of people are still doing it. So with the new awareness we can really still make a difference... really excellent material. I was interested to see the age profile at the

meeting… I think that there is an opportunity for someone of my age to learn a lot with you younger guys… In my mind, you are definitely in the 'one to watch' category!! I look forward to watching your success unfold!"

–David Keane, Bob Proctor Trained Life Coach, Progressive Living, Galway, Ireland

"I thought that your speech was great and a couple of people came to me at the end of the night and said that your talk was really good. The presentation itself was interesting and the look of the presentation was good. Your style of presenting is good and you are very natural."

–Olivia Hayes, President, JCI Galway, Galway, Ireland

"I will admit, I haven't been reading John's e-zine religiously, but it is the only one that I choose to continue my subscription to. I started to pay attention to these emails, and I would open them up to have a look-see. I found the information therein was relevant, easy to understand and follow… I went back and I read some more of them and realized that this wasn't just some meathead spouting regurgitated knowledge. This was a real person, an intelligent person, and one that put himself out there for the world to know about. I read his '39 Things You Should Know About Me…' and saw this was a man not out to impress the masses. Not a man out to become famous. Just a man telling his story, helping people along the way, the best way he knew how. In doing so, he transformed from 'just' a man into a 'great' man."

–Jon McCarty Jr., USA

For more testimonials visit www.JohnMulry.com/testimonials

About the Author

John Mulry is an author, speaker, coach, business 2.0 strategist, and GKIC certified business advisor. He consults with and provides small business owners and entrepreneurial professionals with the systems, strategies and tools they need to attract, convert and retain their ideal clients and unlock the untapped potential in their lives and their businesses faster than they could ever do on their own.

Through his information products, coaching, strategy sessions, private monthly GKIC chapter membership meetings, and educating people on what he calls, "the new rules for local business marketing" mixed with positive change, he instils an expectancy of success rather than failure. He aims to help you achieve more in your life and business in the next 12 months than you could possibly imagine.

Seeing the negative effects not taking care of yourself can have on you and others in your life first-hand drove John to transform his own lifestyle for the better. Turning his focus to helping others change, too, began with fitness, but John soon found out that fitness was just one facet of a bigger problem. People inherently believe and have been conditioned to think that they have to settle for less or are limited in what they can achieve, in life and in business.

With the Expect Success Academy, John aims to show that you can achieve everything you want. He delivers a complete and fully integrated coaching, business, and personally enriching experience that maps out an evolutionary way of getting and living the life you deserve.

John Mulry, MSc

His goal is to be the ultimate one-stop destination for professional and entrepreneurial individuals and organisations that have an interest in or questions about success in business, personal growth, and getting the life you deserve.

John believes that success leaves clues and there is no need to feel like you're "on an island" or alone in your pursuit of personal or business fulfilment. With a rare skill for finding out what it is you need and showing you how to get it, he may challenge your beliefs and may seriously make you question just how far you can go and how much you think you can succeed.

If you go with it, listen, read, and apply the techniques and skills John shows you while keeping an open mind, you will begin down a path to a happier, healthier, and more successful you than you ever thought possible!

For more information on John Mulry, the Expect Success Academy, how you can book John for a keynote speech, join his private monthly membership meeting, or to enquire about how he can help you and your business visit:

www.JohnMulry.com